Youth Leadership Development Workbook

A Guide for Emerging Young Leaders

PUBLISHED BY
NEW LIGHT LEADERSHIP COALITION, INC. (NLLC)
PO Box 66305
BALTIMORE, MARYLAND 21239-6305
1.866.NLLC.INC
WWW.NLLC.ORG

Copyright © 2001-2002 by New Light Leadership Coalition, Inc. (NLLC). All rights reserved. No part of this publication may be reproduced, stored in a retrieval system or transmitted in any form or by any means electronic, mechanical, or otherwise without the prior written permission of the publisher.

ISBN# 0-9716696-0-0

NLLC
PO Box 66305
Baltimore, MD 21239-6305
USA
www.nllc.org

Table of Contents

THE IMPORTANCE OF LEADERSHIP FOR YOUTH
Preface

Leadership is not a privilege; it is a right. Every man, woman, and child has the right to be taught how to be a leader for his or herself and others.

Unfortunately, our attitudes about leaders and leadership have not been expanded even though our present world is undergoing an explosion in both scientific and technological advances. In our society, we are not taught that everyone is a potential leader. What qualifies your parents to be leaders? How about your pastor, your favorite teacher, or that A+ student in your class? We are trained to think that those who wear the title of "leader" do so because of some superhuman, special ability--not fully understanding the very essence of leadership is not on the outside, but on the inside.

There is a need for leadership training for young people, not just adults. Youth today do not have any leaders who we can call our own. There are no young leaders for other youth to admire. The affects of this lack of leadership are just as ineffective as bad leadership. In both conditions, the followers are not guided to where they should be. It is necessary for young people to have the opportunity for leadership training because it improves the person's perception of his or herself, it influences young people to be positive examples for their peers, and it empowers youth to be a major force in the development of the community.

Parents, teachers, and scholars are aware that something is wrong but do not know exactly what the problem is or how to solve it. New Light Leadership Coalition (NLLC)'s leadership training is specifically designed for youth, by youth, to address the desire among young people to become effective leaders. This training changes the perception of a young person by instilling confidence and independence, and uproots the many misconceptions that youth suffer from on a daily basis. Once a young person's eyes are opened to their own leadership potential, the mission to go out in the communities to get others from their present condition of low self-esteem, hopelessness, and despair is born. We want to prove to ourselves and to others the power of our creative energy once it has been guided in the right direction and expended for the right cause.

What is important is that young people become catalysts in the lives of their peers. We understand the need for youth to be positive examples for each other in order to change. NLLC's method influences this change by turning leadership training into a systematic social process. What makes us different is that we are an organization founded by young people. A young person will not learn the potential within self unless they see that potential exemplified by those that they can relate to, which are other young people. This dynamic between youth creates an atmosphere for change.

NLLC believes in training youth for leadership today, because tomorrow will be too late.

-Farajii Rasulallah Muhammad
President & Chairman
New Light Leadership Coalition, Inc. {NLLC}

Copyright © 2001 New Light Leadership Coalition, Inc.   *All Rights Reserved*

INTRODUCTION
How to use this workbook

Thank you for taking the time to start the process of becoming a leader by reading this book. We want you to know a few things before you go on. There are instructions on the proper handling of this material, as there are instructions for anything of value. In order to gain the understanding needed, you must have the **vision** and the **will** to achieve the goals that you are expected to accomplish as a young leader.

This workbook should be used to build your **foundation** to become an inspiration to your peers and others. We hope that you not only read it, but also use it as a reference and a guide to keep you on the path of leadership development. Remember that this workbook is only the beginning. We encourage you to take your study beyond these pages and look deeper into your own thoughts as well as the thoughts of others through our *Suggested Reading List* at the end of each chapter. *Note: All books in the suggested reading lists can be purchased through the NLLC website at **www.nllc.org**.*

We hope that with this book we can invoke a **change**. We want to make a change in your attitude and perception about yourself and the world around you, so you may have an opportunity to live up to your greatest potential and master your destiny by being an effective leader.

Remember that only you have the **power** to achieve your goals.

-Executive Board
New Light Leadership Coalition, Inc.

Youth Leadership Pre-Test

A leader has certain characteristics that make him or her successful. Evaluate yourself on your own personal leadership capabilities by taking the quiz below. Circle the number that corresponds with each statement. Be honest!

	Strongly Disagree	Disagree Somewhat	Agree Somewhat	Strongly Agree
I am comfortable with myself	0	1	2	3
I am a good listener	0	1	2	3
I am a confident person	0	1	2	3
I am self-motivated	0	1	2	3
I am organized	0	1	2	3
I am good at getting my point across	0	1	2	3
I am willing to take on new challenges	0	1	2	3
I am responsible	0	1	2	3
I am not afraid of change	0	1	2	3
People look to me for guidance	0	1	2	3
I can motivate others	0	1	2	3
I think positively	0	1	2	3
I have control of my life	0	1	2	3
I work well with others	0	1	2	3
I am an honest person	0	1	2	3
I have a sincere desire to help others	0	1	2	3
I am good at solving problems	0	1	2	3
I am a risk-taker	0	1	2	3
I follow through with my goals	0	1	2	3
I know my purpose in life	0	1	2	3
Now add up the numbers in each column:	0	_____	_____	_____
Add the column totals to get your total score:	My Total Score_____			

Meaning of Score:

46 – 60 * You are a well-rounded individual well on your way to becoming a leader!

32 – 45 * You have the potential to become a great leader. There are some qualities you want to develop before you are ready to take on leadership roles.

0 – 31 * You may not think you are a leader now, but keep trying to develop your leadership skills. Review the Youth Leadership Development Workbook and take this quiz again at the end of the book.

Copyright © 2001 New Light Leadership Coalition, Inc.   *All Rights Reserved*

CHAPTER 1:
INTRODUCTION TO
LEADERSHIP DEVELOPMENT

TOPICS IN INTRODUCTION TO LEADERSHIP DEVELOPMENT

- Defining Leadership
- Am I a Leader?
- Leadership Qualities
- Types of Leadership
- Principles of Leadership Development

CHAPTER 1: INTRODUCTION TO LEADERSHIP DEVELOPMENT

Key Terms for Introduction to Leadership Development

1. ABILITY a natural or acquired skill or talent

2. AUTHORITY power to influence or command thought, opinion, or behavior

3. CAPACITY innate potential for growth, development, or accomplishment

4. CHANGE the act, process, or result of altering or modifying

5. CHOICE the act of choosing among alternatives; selection

6. DECISION 1. the act of reaching a conclusion 2. the passing of judgment on an issue under consideration

7. DEVELOPMENT the act or process of developing; progressing, growing; evolving

8. GUIDE a person who directs another's conduct or course of life

9. INFLUENCE the act or power of producing an effect without apparent exertion of force or direct exercise of command

10. INTERDEPENDENT a mutually beneficial relationship or arrangement

11. LEAD to guide on a way especially by going in advance; to direct on a course or in a direction (guide, conduct, direct, steer)

12. LEADER one who acts as a change agent in actions or ideas

13. LEADERSHIP the function of acting in the capacity or ability to lead

14. POTENTIAL capable of being or becoming

15. POWER ability to do or act; capability of doing or accomplishing something

DEFINING LEADERSHIP

"Leadership is not when man defines who you are, but when you redefine yourself."
-Farajii Muhammad
President & Chairman
New Light Leadership Coalition, Inc.

How do you define **leadership**? Most people define leadership based on their personal experiences and perceptions of what a leader is. These definitions are usually descriptive of the evidence of leadership, but do not get to the core of the discipline. At the root of leadership is the word **lead**, meaning to **guide** or direct. If **ability** is a natural or acquired skill or talent, what gives us the ability to lead?

We all have the instinct to lead when we are born. As babies we guide ourselves through a new environment and gradually discover our abilities. As we grow older, we learn new and better ways of doing things and make decisions based on our limited knowledge and experience. This innate ability is unique to human beings and gives each of us the potential for leadership. In order to be a leader one must be able to first lead or guide self.

In order to lead, there must be movement from one state to another or **change**. The suffix *–ship* indicates both movement and ability. A **leader** is one who acts as a *change agent* in actions or ideas. In order to be a change agent, or a facilitator of change, a movement from one level of consciousness to another must take place. Challenging the status quo is a requirement of leadership. If we continue to do things the way they have always been done, there is no escalation or growth. Leaders are not afraid to spearhead new movements and challenge old ideas and practices. Exercising the ability or **power** to be a leader is the essence of leadership.

➤ What is leadership to you? Write your definition below:

_____

_____

_____

_____

AM I A LEADER?

We define leadership as *exercising the ability to be a change agent in one's environment*. This means that being a leader requires <u>action</u>. Leadership also requires maximizing your **capacity** and exploring your leadership abilities.

A commonly debated point in the discussion of leadership is the answer to the question: *are leaders born or made?* NLLC believes that leaders are born a*nd then made*. This means that everyone has the **potential** for leadership. Proper training is needed to groom an individual to bring out their leadership abilities. A combination of the preparation and training you receive for taking on leadership roles and the opportunities that present themselves in your lifetime all play a part.

If you think about what makes many of the people we regard as leaders — past and present — there are two things that cross our minds; 1. An important event they played a key role in, and 2. The skills or tactics they used to handle the situation. Below are some examples of some leaders you may have heard of and the defining moments that made history regard them as persons of consequence.

Figure 1.1: Notable Leaders

Person	Critical Event/Role in History	Notable Traits
Martin Luther King, Jr.	March on Washington Civil Rights Movement	Perseverance
John F. Kennedy	Cuban Missile Crisis President of the US	Authority
The Honorable Minister Louis Farrakhan	Million Man March Rebuilding of Nation of Islam	Truth, Character, Consistency
Russell Simmons	Hip Hop Summit Founder of Def Jam Records	Determination, Vision

Many of the aforementioned are also great orators; however, their leadership encompasses so much more than charismatic personality and speeches. Not all of us will be leaders on a grand scale as the CEOs of large corporations or the heads of nations, but we all play a part in our own lives to organize ideas and **influence** others to bring those ideas into existence.

Leaders are not made overnight. It takes time and experience to develop leadership skills. The important thing to remember is that effective leadership requires **development**--the process of progressing, growing, or evolving. No leader that stays stagnant remains a leader. One must enter into this lifelong process of development in order to master the disciplines necessary for leadership.

➢ Name some qualities you think a leader should have:

_____   _____

_____   _____

➢ Name two people who are leaders to you:

_____   _____

LEADERSHIP QUALITIES

All leaders have qualities that make them successful. School principals, leaders of organizations, class presidents, and even the presidents of nations all have similar attributes. Think about your personal skills as you read about the following eleven qualities common to effective leadership.

1. **Creativity** ✦ the ability to find new and innovative solutions for problems

2. **Character** ✦ moral or ethical strength; to always be true to yourself and your values

3. **Commitment** ✦being bound emotionally or intellectually to a course of action or to another person or persons, the ability to stick to your decisions

4. **Confidence** ✦ belief in yourself and your abilities

5. **Courage** ✦ the ability to take initiative and assume risks

6. **Discipline** ✦ orderly conduct and self-control

7. **Organization** ✦ the ability to structure your life and keep tasks and information in order

8. **Optimism** ✦ the ability to see the best possible outcome or dwell on the most hopeful aspects of a situation.

9. **Perseverance** ✦ refusing to quit; willingness to keep goals in sight and work toward them despite obstacles

10. **Understanding** ✦the ability to listen to others and see things from their point of view

11. **Vision** ✦ the ability to visualize one's goals while working to achieve them; foresight

---

WHAT A LEADER IS NOT:

☑ A LEADER IS NOT COMPROMISING

☑ A LEADER IS NOT FEARFUL AND SCARED

☑ A LEADER IS NOT WEAK

☑ A LEADER IS NOT CONFUSED

☑ A LEADER IS NOT SELFISH

☑ A LEADER IS NOT ARROGANT

☑ A LEADER IS NOT IRRESPONSIBLE

TIPS FOR DEVELOPING LEADERSHIP QUALITIES

Below are some suggestions for developing leadership qualities:

> **Creativity -** Think outside of the box. Creativity is as simple as that. Look at all sides of any situation and try things that have not been tried before. Leaders must be creative in their approach. Innovative approaches and new ideas are a part of leadership. To unleash your creativity, try looking at things from a different perspective. If faced with a problem there seems to be no solution for, think about it harder. This may sound simple but it is just that easy. Brainstorming with others helps to come up with ideas you may not have thought of.

> **Character -** Character is moral or ethical strength. Character is not about how others see you, but about how you see yourself. If being truthful is important to you, it will bother you if others think that you are a liar. More importantly, you will not be able to live with yourself if you have been untruthful, even if you get away with it in the eyes of others. True character is the ability to stick to your own values no matter what others may think or say about you. A sign of weak character is changing your views and actions depending on who is around you. What is important to you? To always be true to yourself and your values, you must first identify what your values are. In the Chapter 2, you will explore yourself and identify what your values are. The key to good character is making a commitment to yourself.

> **Commitment -** Commitment in leadership means being able to stay true to what you set out to do. When you are committed, you are conscious of your responsibility to yourself and others. Oftentimes, we decide not to do things because our level of commitment to a cause or goal is weak. Your *desire* to want to develop your leadership skills is causing you to read this book. Your *commitment* to becoming a leader is shown when you follow through with what you learn and apply those things to your life. This shows that desire fuels the will or level of commitment to stick to a task or goal. If you find yourself obligated to do something you later decide not to do, check your motivation. Why did you commit in the first place? Was it your desire or were there external factors that influenced your decision? Sometimes we just need to keep the initial goal in mind to stay committed to our decisions. Stay on track by using friends and family for support. In order to stay committed you should always be in search of new ways to keep yourself motivated.

> **Confidence -** No one can give you confidence. Confidence is the outward reflection of what is inside of you. People will see you as a confident person as a result of an inner feeling of self-worth. The enemy of confidence is self-hatred and the lack of self-esteem. If you lack confidence, you may want to think about why. Is it because of what other people say about you? Have others shaped your self-image? Why have you allowed them do to so? It is difficult to reject the views of others when peer's opinions seem so important. Being secure in yourself and your abilities will help you regain your confidence. What do you do well? What do others recognize you for? Criticism can also damage an individual's confidence if not presented with the right motive. If someone is jealous of you they will try to tear you down with words and through their actions. No matter why kind of criticism you receive, consider it and see it as an opportunity for growth and development. Identifying

your strengths and working to improve your weaknesses will give you the confidence you need for leadership.

➢ **Courage** - Courage is the ability to take initiative and assume risks--to step into the unknown when no one else will. Courage requires vision. It also requires a confidence that is not affected by what others may say or think. While constructive criticism is helpful, do not shy away from making a decision because someone disagrees with you. Leadership is not about popularity; it is about doing what is right regardless to whom or what. If you find yourself afraid of taking an action, evaluate why you are afraid. What is causing your fear? What expected consequence of your action is causing resistance? Decide if you can deal with what will happen after you do something that may seem controversial or unpopular to others. Most great leaders were and are controversial for being against the status quo. In order to be an agent for change you must, in most cases, go against the norm and try something new. Do not be afraid of adversity if you know you are doing what is right.

➢ **Discipline** - Discipline requires order. Disorderly conduct occurs when you do things that are inappropriate. Knowing the right way to do things comes from experience and advice. Learning from your own mistakes and the mistakes of others will make you a more efficient person. Once you learn how to do something efficiently, you have to be able to teach yourself to make those things habitual. They key to discipline is repetition. Doing something over and over again will make it a habit and it will become second nature to you. If there is an order to the way you do things, cultivate that by setting small goals for yourself to be able to maintain that order in your life.

➢ **Organization** - Before tackling the problem of disorganization, it is important to take things one step at a time. Do not discourage yourself by becoming overwhelmed. First, realize what causes you to be disorganized. It is also important to target the aspects of your life where you need better organization. Develop a system for keeping things in order. If you know your room is a mess because of clothes and books and everything else, come up with a system to manage how you take care of your clothing and other belongings. You may want to dedicate one day a week to cleaning your room or even a few minutes out of the day. That is all it takes to organize most things. Also, invest in a planner. Plan and organize your schedule a week in advance if possible, but allow some space for flexibility. Do not make your schedule so rigid that you will not stick to it, but do not give up and abandon the system if you slip up once or twice. You may want to modify your new way of doing things so you can adjust. Be sure to consult your planner at least once a day, preferably in the morning or in the evening before you begin your next day. It does no good to make extensive plans and never look at them. The key to becoming organized is to just do it. Organization of your affairs is an ongoing process that you will constantly revise throughout your life. The habits and methods of organization you adopt in your personal life will reflect in anything else that you do--including running a business or an organization.

➢ **Optimism -** The kind of person you are can determine how successful you will become. It is important that you recognize both your strengths and weaknesses. Try

Copyright © 2001 New Light Leadership Coalition, Inc.   *All Rights Reserved*

to improve a little each day. You may have noticed that your day goes better when you feel good about yourself. This is an *optimistic* or positive attitude. Leaders are optimists. They have to be in order to see opportunities where others only see roadblocks. Remember that apparent failures are learning opportunities. Learn from mistakes to improve future performance.

➢ **Perseverance -** Try to approach new situations with a different attitude. Can you think of a time when you were confronted with change? How did you handle it? Why did you respond the way you did? By analyzing how you respond to things, you can determine your motivations. Some things will change that we want to stay the same. Try to have a proactive attitude about these things by realizing that you have the power to control your response to the situation even if you do not have the ability to change the circumstances. By focusing on your core values and becoming a better person, you do not empower things outside of you to affect you and disturb your peace. *The choices we make are our own. We cannot blame anyone else for our actions.*

➢ **Understanding -** As your knowledge and experience increase, so does your understanding. The ability to act on knowledge and experience is what constitutes wisdom. In order to make wise decisions and interact better with other people, a proper understanding of what you are dealing with is necessary. You must learn to put yourself in the other person's shoes. Always try to think in terms of another person's needs and desires. If you have a member of your organization that is slacking in their duties, they may not respond to you yelling at them and telling them why you are right. Try to think about why they may be performing badly. Is there a deeper personal problem you don't know about? Are they unable to perform their job because they lack the skills but are ashamed to tell anyone? Maybe they don't care at all. In any case, finding out what motivates a person will help you have a better understanding of why people do what they do.

➢ **Vision -** Visualize where you want to end up. If you are elected the president of your student government or another organization, how do you see the organization changing as a result of your leadership? What is the ultimate goal? Think about where you want to go until you get a clear picture in your mind. Remind yourself of your vision everyday. One technique you may try is having a phrase that represents your vision in plain sight so that you see it everyday. This will keep your mind on the end result and give you the ability to take action steps towards your ultimate goal.

Complete Activities 1 & 2 at the end of this chapter before continuing to the next page.

TYPES OF LEADERSHIP

There are many types of leadership. The first and most basic type is self-leadership, or the ability to control and direct yourself throughout life. This involves being a decision-maker about what is best for your personal development. Once you master self and become an independent thinker, you can evolve to one of the next types of leadership. As the chart below shows, the effect of each type of leadership has a different scale--with the global leader being the one with the greatest impact on others.

Self – Control and direction of oneself
Group/Team – Guidance of a small group or team, facilitator
Organizational – Provides vision for entire organization or large group
Political – Public leadership for a city, state, or nation.
Global – Leaders whose ideas transcend culture and nationalism and have a lasting effect on the entire world.

Figure 1.2: Types of Leadership

The second type of leadership is at the group or team level. A team leader exists as a guide for a small group of individuals. At this level of leadership, there is **interdependence** or a mutually beneficial situation for all involved. No one is completely independent or dependent on the other's function--everyone contributes something to the group. Organizational leadership implies authority over a large group or an organization. This includes businesses, schools, or any other institution with its own rules and culture. Political leadership is at the city, state, or national level. These leaders are elected into office or appointed, just as organizational leaders, but function to serve the entire public and not just one select group. Political leaders are sometimes limited in function because they are accountable to such a diverse group of people with varying needs. The final type of leadership discussed here is global leadership. Global leaders' have ideals that transcend all barriers. Some examples of global leaders include Ghandi, Albert Einstein, the Honorable Minister Louis Farrakhan, and Martin Luther King, Jr. Global leaders are usually not fully understood or appreciated during the time in which they live because they are so far ahead of others. Most leaders of this type have grown to a level where others will fulfill their ideas and missions in future generations.

Figure 1.3: Hierarchy of Leadership Types

PRINCIPLES OF LEADERSHIP DEVELOPMENT

NLLC approaches leadership development based on the following principles:

Know Yourself

An innate potential for leadership exists within every human being. Everyone is inclined to leadership—first of themselves and then others. **Personal development** will reveal these hidden abilities and identify key values. The proper knowledge of self is essential for mastery of leadership. Through training one can be guided to strengthen weaknesses, maximize strengths, and reach their full potential.

Learn About Others and the World Around You

Leadership implies both a self and group dynamic. Through **social development**, one obtains the tools necessary to understand and communicate with others. **Educational development** involves the personal quest for knowledge and learning from life experience.

Use Your Resources Effectively

After gaining knowledge of the environment, tools necessary to become a change agent in that environment are needed. Leaders must master their human, financial, and material resources. **Economic development** enables one to master their financial resources. **Political development** is the art of using material and human resources efficiently for the good of the whole. **Technological development** is an integral part of leadership in today's ever-changing and competitive environment. Finally, building on all of these things comes **organizational development**. Mastering the use of resources will enable you to be successful in organizational development.

Out of these principles, seven areas of development are derived—*personal, social, educational, economic, political, technological,* and *organizational* development. This workbook will explore each of these areas of focus as they relate to leadership development.

Copyright © 2001 New Light Leadership Coalition, Inc.   *All Rights Reserved*

SEVEN AREAS OF DEVELOPMENT

We realize that leadership encompasses many things, and have identified seven areas of development to create a holistic approach to this discipline.

PERSONAL DEVELOPMENT

In order to be an effective leader, one must look to the leader within. A proper knowledge of self and a higher power are key in developing leadership skills. This knowledge is enlightening, empowering, and essential for all human beings to attain success. This portion of the workbook will help you delve into what makes you unique and the natural leadership capabilities within.

SOCIAL DEVELOPMENT

Leaders must adopt social responsibility. Community service, respect to our elders, and contributing to an environment of progression and unity are essential for emerging leaders. Understanding and respect for culture, public speaking, communication skills, conflict resolution, and team building are covered under social development.

EDUCATIONAL DEVELOPMENT

We should strive for the best in all educational endeavors. Understanding that education goes beyond the classroom and preparing to advance formal education are both important. Job and career planning, exploring learning styles, and effective study habits are reviewed in this chapter.

ECONOMIC DEVELOPMENT

Leaders must be able to plan, budget, and manage funds. Good money management is the stepping-stone to economic empowerment through commerce and the pooling of resources to start new ventures. We must learn to support community businesses and realize our buying power. Aspects of financial planning and entrepreneurship are discussed in chapter five.

POLITICAL DEVELOPMENT

A proper understanding of the political process and how it affects our community is necessary. Registering to vote and being educated about our government are key. This section describes ways youth can get involved in the politics and challenges many misconceptions about political process.

TECHNOLOGICAL DEVELOPMENT

Today we live in a technologically advanced society. Media and technology effect virtually every aspect of human life each day. It is vital that every young person learns how to master technology to become competitive members of society. Technological development gives an overview of vital issues in the area technology such as the digital divide and access to resources.

ORGANIZATIONAL DEVELOPMENT

Building on the above six areas of development lies the foundation for starting or improving any organization or project. NLLC will aid in organizational development of its members and affiliates by providing start-up and evaluation tools for strategic planning.

Copyright © 2001 New Light Leadership Coalition, Inc.   *All Rights Reserved*

CHAPTER 1 REVIEW QUESTIONS

1. Define *leader*.

    _____

    _____

    _____

2. What is the most influential type of leader? Why?

    _____

    _____

    _____

3. True or False--Only certain people are born to be leaders. Explain your answer.

    _____

    _____

    _____

4. What are the principles of leadership development?

    *   _____

    *   _____

    *   _____

5. What advice would you give to a person who wants to increase their level of understanding?

    _____

    _____

    _____

CHAPTER 1 ACTIVITIES

1. List three (3) leadership qualities you already have:

    a. _____

    b. _____

    c. _____

2. List three (3) leadership qualities you plan to work to develop:

    a. _____

    b. _____

    c. _____

    d. How will you work to develop these qualities?

_____

_____

_____

_____

3.   Name a leader you know. Write their name below:

_____

What type of leader is he/she?

        Self   Group/Team   Organizational   Political   Global

    a. What qualities make them a leader? _____

_____

_____

_____

    b. How does their leadership influence others? _____

_____

_____

_____

    c. What do you admire about this person? _____

_____

_____

_____

CHAPTER 1 PROJECTS

1. Complete the **Youth Leadership Development Workbook** and take the Youth Leadership Post-test.

2. Read one of the suggested readings below and answer the following questions:

   Book Title: _____

   a. What did you learn by reading this book?

   _____

   _____

   _____

   _____

   b. Was it helpful? Why or why not?

   _____

   _____

   _____

   _____

   c. Would you recommend this book to others? Explain.

   _____

   _____

   _____

SUGGESTED READING FOR CHAPTER 1

1. Secrets of Effective Leadership: A Practical Guide to Success by Fred A. Manske

2. The Leader in You by Dale Carnegie

3. Martin Luther King, Jr., on Leadership: Inspiration & Wisdom for Challenging Times by Donald T. Phillips

4. 7 Habits of Highly Effective People by Stephen Covey

5. Leadership Secrets of Attila the Hun by Wess Roberts

CHAPTER 2: PERSONAL DEVELOPMENT

TOPICS IN PERSONAL DEVELOPMENT

- Who Am I?
- Goal Setting
- Problem Solving & Decision Making

CHAPTER 2: PERSONAL DEVELOPMENT

 ## Key Terms for Personal Development

1. **AWARENESS** the state of being informed; alert; knowledgeable, conscious; having knowledge

2. **FEAR** a feeling of disquiet or apprehension

3. **GOAL** the result or achievement toward which effort is directed; aim

4. **GROWTH** 1. size or stage of development 2. development from a simpler to a more complex stage

5. **INDIVIDUAL** distinguished by special, singular, or markedly personal characteristics;

6. **LOVE** 1. a feeling of strong attachment induced by that which delights or commands admiration. 2. preeminent kindness or devotion to another; affection; devotion. 3. unselfish loyal and benevolent concern

7. **MISSION** an assigned or self-imposed duty or task

8. **PASSION** a strong liking or desire for or devotion to some activity, object, or concept

9. **PERSONALITY** the sum total of the physical, mental, emotional, and social characteristics of an individual.

10. **PLAN** a scheme or method of acting, doing, proceeding, making, etc., developed in advance

11. **PURPOSE** the reason for which something exists 2. an intended or desired result; end; aim; goal.

12. **SELF** the uniting principle underlying all subjective experience.

13. **SELF-HATE** the inability to love oneself due to a distorted perception of reality

14. **SKILL** the ability, coming from one's knowledge, practice, aptitude, etc., to do something well

15. **UNIQUE** 1. existing as the only one or as the sole example; single; solitary in type or characteristics 2. . having no like or equal; unparalleled; incomparable

16. **VALUE** a principle, standard, or quality considered worthwhile or desirable

---

WHO AM I?

The concept of **self** refers to the unique attributes and qualities that comprise an **individual**. These attributes all come out of our own personal and subjective experience as we move through life. Many things affect our self-image. Negative images and experiences that may not be rooted in reality sometimes determine how we see ourselves. Each individual is **unique** meaning there is no one else like you on the planet--even if you have an identical twin. Everyone has a purpose in life. If you do not know what your purpose is then you will lead a misguided life and will be unable to focus on one specific **goal**. Finding out your purpose is a process that begins with self-examination.

Our self-image is determined by what we think about ourselves and sometimes by what others think about us. If a child is constantly told that they are worthless, he or she may grow up to fulfill that self-destructive path in life. The truth is each of us is born for a reason. When we understand the importance of self and how we relate to the world around us, we can interact appropriately with the outside world.

SELF-RESPECT

Self-awareness should bring about a respect and love of self. Spirituality is an important part of self-respect because it causes us to reflect on that which is greater than us. When we take the time to realize that we did not give life to ourselves, we are humbled and can learn to treat ourselves better and have a true respect for life. We are concerned about the respect of our parents, children, co-workers, friends, and others--but what about ourselves? You must love yourself before anyone else can love you.

There is nothing more important to our emotional, psychological, or spiritual well being than **love**. It is a vital part of any **growth** process. We need self-love and self-respect so that we can interact with and view others properly. To be loved is to feel accepted and have a sense of belonging.

The common misconception about love is that it is a feeling. Love is not just the romantic or warm feeling one may have for a mate or family member. Love is not an emotion—it is the creative force from which everything is born. The word love is a verb, which implies that in order to love anything there must be action and not just lip profession. To love is to treat another person with devotion and the utmost respect. Unconditional love means that no matter what someone else does or what we perceive is done *to* us, our hearts remain pure and able to treat another human being with the same devotion and respect we demand for ourselves. Unconditional love of self means that regardless of what we do wrong, we can still see the good in ourselves and begin to improve upon our shortcomings.

Complete Activity 1 at the end of this chapter before continuing to the next page.

SELF-HATRED

The opposite of self-respect is **self-hate**. Self-hatred immobilizes an individual and causes him or her to place more value on others than on self. This principle is propagated through society and in our personal lives. People of color have a more difficult road to self-awareness because many things--both consciously and subconsciously--continue to teach us that we are not destined for greatness when quite the opposite is true. This is sometimes called *the Willie Lynch Syndrome,* named after a slavemaster credited with the development of the slavemaking process.

Read the following excerpt from *Let's Make a Slave.* As you read, think about the effect that this mentality has on people of color today.

Let's Make a Slave
"The Origin and Development of a Social Being Called 'The Negro'"
by Willie Lynch

Let us make a slave. What do we need?
First of all we need a black Negro man, a pregnant Negro woman and her baby Negro boy. Second, we will use the same basic principle that we use in breaking a horse, combined with some more sustaining factors. We reduce them from their natural state in nature; whereas nature provides them with the natural capacity to take care of their needs and the needs of their offspring, we break that natural string of independence from them and thereby create a dependency state so that we maybe able to get from them useful production for our business and pleasure.

CARDINAL PRINCIPLE FOR MAKING A NEGRO
For fear that our future generations may not understand the principle of breaking both horses and men, we lay down the art. For, if we are to sustain our basic economy we must break both of the beasts together, the Negro and the horse. We understand that short range planning in economics results in periodic economic chaos, so that, to avoid turmoil in the economy, it requires us to have breadth and depth in long range comprehensive planning, articulating both skill and sharp perception. We lay down the following principles for long-range comprehensive economic planning:
1.   Both horse and engross are no good to the economy in the wild or natural state
2.   Both must be broken and tied together for orderly production.
3.   For orderly futures, special and particular attention must be paid to the female and the youngest offspring.
4.   Both must be crossbred to produce a variety and division of labor.
5.   Both must taught to respond to a peculiar new language.
6.   Psychological and physical instruction of containment must be created for both.

We hold the above six cardinals as truths to be self-evident, based upon following discourse concerning the economics of breaking and tying the horse and Negro together...all inclusive of the six principles laid down above. NOTE: Neither principles alone will suffice for good economics. All principles must be employed for the orderly good of the nation. Accordingly, both a wild horse and a wild or natural Negro is dangerous even if captured, for they will have the tendency to seek their customary freedom, and, in doing so, might kill you in your sleep. You cannot rest. They sleep while you are awake and are awake while you are asleep. They are dangerous near the family house and it requires too much labor to watch them away from the house. Above all you cannot get them to work in this natural state. Hence, both the horse and the Negro must be broken, that is break them from one form of mental life to another, keep the body and take the mind. In other words, break the will to resist.

Now the breaking process in the same for the horse and the Negro, only slightly varying in degrees. But as we said before, you must keep your eye focused on the female and the offspring of the horse and the Negro. A brief discourse in offspring development will shed light on the key to sound economic principle. Pay little attention to the generation of original breaking but concentrate on future generations. Therefore, if you break the female, she will break the offspring in its early years of development and, when the offspring is old enough to work, she will deliver it up to you. For her normal female protective tendencies will have been lost in the original breaking process. For example, take the case of the wild stud horse, a female horse and an already infant horse and compare the breaking process with two captured Negro males in their natural state, a pregnant Negro woman with her infant offspring. Take the stud horse, break him for limited containment. Completely break the female horse until she becomes very gentle whereas you or anybody

---

can ride her in comfort. Breed the mare until you have the desired offspring. Then you can turn the stud to freedom until you need him again. Train the female horse whereby she will eat out of your hand, and she will train the infant horse to eat of your hand also.

When it comes to breaking the uncivilized Negro, use the same process, but vary the degree and step up the pressure so as to do a complete reversal of the mind. Take the meanest and most restless Negro, strip him of his clothes in front of the remaining Negroes, the female, and the Negro infant, tar and feather him, tie each leg to a different horse faced in opposite directions, set him a fire and beat both horses to pull him apart in front of the remaining Negroes. The nest step is to take a bullwhip and beat the remaining Negro male to the point of death in front of the female and the infant. Don't kill him. But put the fear of God in him, for he can be useful for future breeding. . .

CONTROLLED LANGUAGE
Crossbreeding completed, for further severance from their original beginning, we must completely annihilate the mother tongue of both the Negro and the new mule and institute a new language that involves the new life's work of both. You know, language is a peculiar institution. It leads to the heart of people. The more a foreigner knows about the language of another country the more he is able to move through all levels of that society. Therefore, if the foreigner is an enemy of the country, to the extent that he knows the body of the language, to that extent is the country vulnerable to attack or invasion of a foreign culture. For example, you take the slave, if you teach him all about your language, he will know all your secrets, and he is then no more a slave, for you can't fool him any longer and having a fool is one of the basic ingredients of and incidents to the making of the slavery system.

Note: The word Negro is used as a substitute for the more offensive language of the original speech.

Reaction to "Let's Make a Slave"

- Do you think the system described in *Let's Make a Slave* still applies in modern America? Why or why not?

_____

_____

_____

_____

- After reading this excerpt, do you think that culture is an important part of self-awareness? Explain.

_____

_____

_____

IMPORTANCE OF FAMILY HISTORY

Your family history will reveal things about your **values**, motivation, and overall health. If alcoholism, depression, or heart disease run in your family, you could be prone to these risks and should be mindful of those weaknesses. Another thing you can learn from your family history is the different cultures in your background. Most of us will find that our families have rich cultural backgrounds with different types of people from different places. Understanding more about the people in our own families will give us a better perspective from which to view the cultures of others. A family tree can help you trace important information about your parents, grandparents, and the generations before them.

Each of our families has a unique story. Finding out about your family will teach you some things about yourself and your immediate family. The things we learn from our families can influence and determine our values.

MY VALUES

An important part of self-discovery is determining what your values are. What matters to you defines your values. A value is a principle, standard, or quality to live by. Many of our values come from our culture, society, and upbringing. The standards we live by affect the way we view the world around us and dictate our actions.

What is important to me?

Values are the things that are intrinsically important to you. You would not be who you are without honoring them. When you live in accordance with your values, your life is fulfilling and everything falls into place. When you do not live by your values or are unaware of what they are, life is boring, dull, irritating, and frustrating. Others are able to pull you in many different directions. Oftentimes, the things that are the most important to you are the least obvious. You could not imagine your life without them but probably take it for granted that those things will always be there. With definition of your values it is easier to identify what is or is not working in any given situation.

Imagine a person who has a value called humor, but is not conscious of it, and is living with someone who never laughs. They may feel disenchanted with the relationship and not know why, until they recognize that humor is a part of their identity and they may feel their humor is suppressed around that person.

When you have a clearer sense of your values, you will more immediately recognize situations, people and things that will enhance and reinforce who you are. Your decisions are made more easily and are based on a personal foundation. Values serve as a reference point when prioritizing actions, commitments, and goals. What motivates you? Is it genuine desire or **fear** of a consequence? Identifying your values is a fascinating process that occurs over time.

Copyright © 2001 New Light Leadership Coalition, Inc.   *All Rights Reserved*

Identifying Your Values

While defining your values is a process, we can begin to identify them by thinking about what is important to us. Most of us have values as it relates to the following things:

♦ Power	♦ Spirituality/Religion
♦ Family	♦ Knowledge
♦ Success	♦ Relationships
♦ Stability & Security	♦ Creativity & Exploration
♦ Role of the Female	♦ Role of the Male
♦ Social Life	♦ Helping Others

To begin identifying your values, write down the five things that are most important to you from the list above. Feel free to include things that may not be included in the list.

1. _____

2. _____

3. _____

4. _____

5. _____

Now, write down your ideal of each of these five things. For example, if you selected power as one of the things most important to you, how do you define your power? Is it important to have power in the workplace, or is your power having control of your household? If you said relationships were important, what kind of relationships do you want to model in your life? Is it important to you to be truthful in relationships or to settle down at a certain age?

Write an explanation for each of your values in the spaces provided below.

1.
2.

3.
4.
5.

YOUR PERSONAL MISSION STATEMENT

The first step in goal setting is defining your **mission**. A mission is an assigned or self-imposed duty or task. A mission statement provides insight into **passion** and **purpose**. A passion is defined as a strong liking, desire for, or devotion to something. Your purpose is your reason for being. The key to writing your personal mission statement is wrapped up in your passion and purpose in life.

There are several ways to go about writing your personal mission statement. It can be as broad or as specific as you want it to be. It may be hard for you to answer the question *what do you want to do with your life?*, so developing a mission statement for the next five to ten years may seem less intimidating and be more practical. Try the following techniques to develop your personal mission statement.

Introspection

To identify your passion, think about the following things: What are your strengths? What are your weaknesses or things you would like to improve about yourself? What would you do with your life if money were not an issue? What would you still do even if you weren't paid to do it? What is the first thing you think about in the morning? What do you look forward to? If you had to give everything away but one thing, what would you keep?

The key to finding out your purpose is self-study and solitude. When your friends and family are not around and you are alone in your room or taking a walk by yourself, where are your thoughts? What do you do? When no none else is there, you can listen to yourself and discover things that may be shielded or hidden to "fit-in" or interact with others.

Envisioning

Think about where you want to be five or even ten years from now. How old are you? Where do you live? What are you driving? Do you have a family? If so, how many children? Where are you working? What do you do in your spare time? Some of these questions should get you thinking about your future self and a picture of that future reality should begin to become clearer.

Values

Identify your core values. What is important to you? Think of it in terms of defining the progress you want to make in certain aspects of your life. For example, your career is important to you so decide how you want to conduct your professional life. Are you bossy, withdrawn, or a team player? How do you want your personal life to progress? Are you a good friend and family member? What about your spiritual life? Do you want to strive to become a better person? Think about all of these things and write down the standards that you want to adhere to in each area of your life.

Look Through a Different Lens

Look at yourself through the eyes of others. How do others you want others to see you? Would they say you are smart, funny, or cruel? Think about what your family members, friends, classmates, teachers, or someone who just met you would say if they were asked to name one thing that describes you. While others are not always right about their impressions of you, those who are closest to you will reveal things that may not have occurred to you. Ask your friends and family to tell you who you are in one word. Their answers may surprise you and give you a different perspective of yourself.

Benefits of Writing Your Personal Mission Statement

1. It forces you to think deeply about <u>your</u> life and identify what is really important to you.

2. It forces you to clarify and express your deepest values and aspirations.

3. It makes your values become a part of you rather than something you just thought about once.

4. Integrating your personal mission statement into your weekly planning and goal setting gives you a way to keep that vision constantly before you.

Figure 2.1: Benefits of Writing a Mission Statement

You may be thinking: *What should my mission statement look like? How long should it be? What should it say?* That is your decision; however, keep in mind that your mission statement should reveal something about your values, strengths and/or weaknesses, and **personality**. The reader of your mission statement should be able to figure out easily who you are, what you are about, and what your plans for the future are.

Complete Activities 2 & 3 at the end of this chapter before continuing to the next page.

Copyright © 2001 New Light Leadership Coalition, Inc.   *All Rights Reserved*

GOAL SETTING

Now that you have written your personal mission statement, you can set goals to help you fulfill your mission. A **goal** is the result or achievement of a direct effort. In short, goal is something you aim to accomplish.

WHY SET GOALS?

Without clearly defined goals, you have no aim or purpose. Goal setting will help you manage your time more effectively. As you begin to take on more responsibilities, your time will be demanded more and more. This requires that you become more aware of how you spend your time and learn to manage time well. Here are some signs that you manage your time inefficiently:

Signs of Poor Time Management
- Rushing
- Nonproductive
- Missing deadlines
- Not enough time for rest and relaxation
- Feeling overwhelmed
- Procrastination
- Disorganization

In order to get the most out of your time, you have to set realistic goals and stick to a plan of action. If you have a large project, break it down into smaller goals – or objectives – that you can complete in a relatively short time period. Take the time to celebrate the accomplishment of small goals and reward yourself with something special.

GOAL SETTING MODEL

The following goal setting model can be used for personal issues and for goal setting for organizations or projects. When approaching goal setting, it is important to remember the following:
- ◆ Break down large projects into small tasks
- ◆ Set goals that are practical and attainable for all activities

Overall, there are five steps to goal setting: defining your goal, setting your objectives, executing your action items, charting your outcomes, and evaluating the end result of your **plan**.

Goal - *What is my overall purpose? What do I want to accomplish?*

First, you set the goal. The goal should be something that you know you can accomplish. Avoid perfectionism in goal setting. If you never achieve what

Figure 2.2: Goal Setting Model

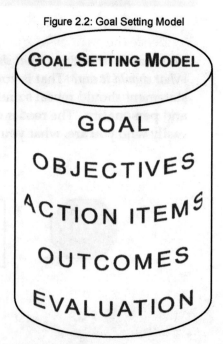

you set out to do, it will only discourage you from setting goals in the future. Set one small goal at a time. Goals should have a deadline, whether it is a specific date or a number of days or weeks. Short-term goals are things that can be completed within one year, while long-term goals will take more than a year to complete. Goals are clear, concise statements that convey what you hope to achieve.

Objectives - *What are the measurable outcomes of this goal?*

What will be the result that shows you completed your goal? For instance, if your goal is to develop your courage, your objective might be to do three things that you are afraid to do. Objectives must be measurable in some quantity. It could be in the number of times something is done, the frequency with which you do something, or how many things are changed as a result of your goal. Objectives are not vague and must be completed in the timeline determined by your goal. Usually, two or three objectives are sufficient to accomplish a goal. If you find yourself setting more than five objectives, consider breaking down your goal into two or more separate goals. If it is an objective for a project or organization, you might decide to recruit 100 members by the end of the year or to sell $500 worth of tickets for a talent show.

Action Items - *What specific actions must I take to fulfill my objectives?*

Action items describe what you will do to achieve your objectives. This is when you get specific about the actions you will take. If it is a personal goal, think about what you will do on a daily basis during the time period of completion of your goal. What will you do each day to work towards your goal? If it is an action item for a project or an organization, think about what people will be involved and what specific duties must be performed to make the project successful. You may determine a certain number of meetings must be held or chart all tasks that must be done.

Outcomes - *What happened? Were the outcomes expected or unexpected?*

Visualize the results of your activity. What will happen? The outcome is the evidence the goal was fulfilled. For example, let's say your goal is to increase the number of students involved in community service on campus and your objective is to sign up 50 students for your new project. A sensible outcome may be that 500 community service hours are performed on campus (10 hours per student) during the school year. Your outcomes should also reflect the time line specified by your goals and objectives--don't use a far-fetched statement that sounds more like a vision than an attainable outcome.

Evaluation - *Did I meet my goal? Why or why not? How can I improve my approach to this goal?*

This is a very important phase in planning and goal setting. Did you meet your goal? Was the method used (activities) effective? Evaluation causes you to reflect on the successes and failure of your plan of action. During the evaluation, it is important to record both the positive and negative impressions of everyone involved to help with future efforts. When evaluating a personal goal, think about your follow-through. Were you able to stick to your plan? Why or why not? A thorough evaluation is critical to your future success.

SAMPLE GOAL SETTING MODEL

Goal: I will become more organized.

What has stopped me from accomplishing this goal?
I have been procrastinating.

Objective 1
- Plan my daily and weekly activities for a month

Action Items
- Buy a planner
- Write down homework assignments in planner
- Make a "TO DO" List for each day and week
- Review my "TO DO" List each morning

Objective 2
- Straighten out my desk and work area

Action Items
- Sort miscellaneous papers using folders and desk organizers
- Use desk organizers for incoming mail and papers
- Keep my work area clean for a month

Outcomes
- My desk and work area will be organized
- My weekly activities will be planned for the next month

Evaluation
I have successfully planned my activities for the month. I only missed a few days of reviewing my TO DO List. I was not successful at keeping my work area clean for the month. The next time I will devote a few minutes after school each day to sort my new mail and papers.

Follow-up (New Goal)
Maintain my schedule and work area.

Figure 2.3: Sample Goal Setting Model

PROBLEM SOLVING

No matter what goals and plans we set for ourselves, there will always be obstacles. They are expected and must be handled before they handle you. Oftentimes, the only thing you are able to control about a situation is your response or attitude when approaching that situation.

THE PROBLEM SOLVING CYCLE

You should approach all decisions and problems with a rational mind. Emotions can cloud your thinking and force you to make unintelligent choices. One decision can indeed change your life, so be careful when you are faced with an important one.

Follow these steps when confronted with a problem or decision:

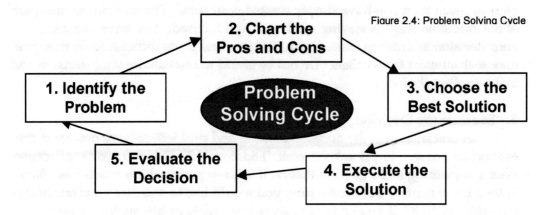

Figure 2.4: Problem Solving Cycle

1. Identify the problem

This may sound basic and even unnecessary, but it is the single most important factor when trying to solve a problem or make a decision. The most common error that occurs when trying to solve a situation is not accurately defining the problem. A child may not be doing well in a particular class, but math may not be the problem. He or she may have to work everyday after school, preventing him or her from being able to study. This could cause the student's grades to fall even if they do have an aptitude for math. The problem here is then a financial problem as opposed to an academic problem or an issue with the student's intelligence.

Once the problem is properly identified, you can then begin to work on the solution.

2. Chart the Pros and Cons

This too may sound basic but many of us fail to approach decision-making in this manner. We simply think about it and weigh options in our minds when making decisions. Sit down and write out the advantages (pros) and disadvantages (cons) of each alternative. This will give you a better picture of what you actually gain by choosing one over the other.

3. Choose the Best Solution

After you identify the pros and cons, you can accurately place value on each possible action. This will not be easy, but at least you have a better model to look at to be able to make your decision. Each choice you make will involve *sacrifice*; you will have to give up one thing in order to do the other.

Take time to decide how valuable each advantage is, and how important each disadvantage is. If deciding whether or not to take an 8:00 a.m. class, you may consider that you almost never get up that early. If you are placed in a situation where that is the only section open, what do you do? The disadvantage of being put behind in your major and having to graduate later or take summer classes may outweigh having to wake up a little earlier in the morning. You may decide to sacrifice staying up late to take the class.

4. Execute the Solution

You have made your decision, now you have to follow through with it. Sometimes good intentions are not backed up with action. If you fail to act on your decision then you have simply wasted your time. The most important part of the execution stage is staying motivated and focused. You have to stick to your decision in order to make it work. If you find it too difficult to do this, you may seek support from others. Do not be afraid to re-evaluate your decision and make another choice.

5. Evaluate the Decision

A crucial step in the decision-making and problem solving process is the evaluation phase. Simply ask yourself, 'Did it work?' This is important because even if something looks good in theory, if it is not practical it is worthless. Back to the idea of the 8:00 am class—sure, you would like to sacrifice your late nights, but will you do it? If you know you work late nights or like staying up late talking to friends, you know you will not wake up that early. If it does not work, go back to square one and try again. This time, you will have more experience and will be able to make a wiser decision.

CHAPTER 2 REVIEW QUESTIONS

1. Define "self." _____

   _____

   _____

2. What is a goal? _____

   _____

   _____

3. Is it important to set goals? Why or why not? _____

   _____

   _____

4. Why is it important to know your family history? _____

   _____

   _____

5. What are the benefits of writing a personal mission statement? _____

   _____

   _____

6. What is the most important step in problem solving? Why? _____

   _____

   _____

   _____

CHAPTER 2 ACTIVITIES

1. Personality Test
The following test is just for fun but it can be very accurate. Take this test to learn about your personality.

1. When do you feel your best?
  (a) in the morning
  (b) during the afternoon
  (c) late at night

2. You usually walk. . .
  (a) fairly fast, with long steps
  (b) fairly fast, with short, quick steps
  (c) less fast head up
  (d) less fast, head down
  (e) very slowly

3. When talking to people you
  (a) stand with your arms folded
  (b) have your hands clasped
  (c) have one or both your hands on your hips
  (d) touch or push the person to whom you are talking
  (e) play with your ear, touch your chin, or smooth your hair

4. When relaxing, you sit with
  (a) your knees bent with your legs neatly side by side
  (b) your legs crossed
  (c) your legs stretched out or straight
  (d) one leg curled under you

5. When something really amuses you, you react with
  (a) a big, appreciative laugh
  (b) a laugh, but not a loud one
  (c) a quiet chuckle
  (d) a sheepish smile

6. When you go to a party or social gathering you
  (a) make a loud entrance so everyone notices you
  (b) make a quiet entrance, looking around for someone you know
  (c) make the quietest entrance, trying to stay unnoticed

7. You're working very hard, concentrating hard, and you're interrupted. Do you..
  (a) welcome the break
  (b) feel extremely irritated
  (c) vary between these two extremes

8. Which of the following colors do you like most?
  (a) red or orange
  (b) black
  (c) yellow or light blue
  (d) green
  (e) dark blue or purple
  (f) white
  (g) brown or gray

9. When you are in bed at night, in those last few moments before going to sleep, you lie
  (a) stretched out on your back
  (b) stretched out face down on your stomach
  (c) on your side, slightly curled
  (d) with your head on one arm
  (e) with your head under the covers

10. You often dream that you are
  (a) falling
  (b) fighting or struggling
  (c) searching for something or somebody
  (d) flying or floating
  (e) you usually have dreamless sleep
  (f) your dreams are always pleasant

SCORING:
1. (a) 2 (b) 4 (c) 6   2. (a) 6 (b) 4 (c) 7 (d) 2 (e) 1
3. (a) 4 (b) 2 (c) 5 (d) 7 (e) 6   4. (a) 4 (b) 6 (c) 2 (d) 1
5. (a) 6 (b) 4 (c) 3 (d) 5 (e) 2   6. (a) 6 (b) 4 (c) 2
7. (a) 6 (b) 2 (c) 4   8. (a) 6 (b) 7 (c) 5 (d) 4 (e) 3 (f) 2 (g) 1
9. (a) 7 (b) 6 (c) 4 (d) 2 (e) 1   10. (a) 4 (b) 2 (c) 3 (d) 5 (e) 6 (f) 1

Add up the total number of points.   **My Total Score _____**

Copyright © 2001 New Light Leadership Coalition, Inc.   *All Rights Reserved*

Meaning of Score

OVER 60 POINTS: Others see you as someone they should "handle with care" You're seen as vain, self-centered, and who is extremely dominant. Others may admire you, wishing they could be more like you, but don't always trust you, hesitating to become too deeply involved with you.

51 TO 60 POINTS: Others see you as an exciting, highly volatile, rather impulsive personality; a natural leader, who's quick to make decisions, though not always the right ones. They see you as bold and adventuresome, someone who will try anything once; someone who takes chances and enjoys an adventure. They enjoy being in your company because of the excitement you radiate.

41 TO 50 POINTS: Others see you as fresh, lively, charming, amusing, practical, and always interesting; someone who's constantly in the center of attention, but sufficiently well-balanced not to let it go to their head. They also see you as kind, considerate, and understanding; someone who'll always cheer them up and help them out.

31 TO 40 POINTS: Others see you as sensible, cautious, careful & practical. They see you as clever, gifted, or talented, but modest...Not a person who makes friends too quickly or easily, but someone who's extremely loyal to friends you do make and who expect the same loyalty in return. Those who really get to know you realize it takes a lot to shake your trust in your friends, but equally that it takes you a long time to get over it if that trust is ever broken...

21 TO 30 POINTS: Your friends see you as painstaking and fussy. They see you as very cautious, extremely careful, a slow and steady plodder. It'd really surprise them if you ever did something impulsively or on the spur of the moment, expecting you to examine everything carefully from every angle and then, usually decide against it. They think this reaction is caused partly by your careful nature.

UNDER 21 POINTS: People think you are shy, nervous, and indecisive, someone who needs looking after, who always wants someone else to make the decisions & who doesn't want to get involved with anyone or anything. They see you as a worrier who always sees problems that don't exist. Some people think you're boring. Only those who know you well know that you aren't.

Personality Test Questions:

a. Were you surprised by your results?   YES   NO   SOMEWHAT

b. Do you think the results of this test are accurate? Why or why not?

_____

_____

_____

c. Did this test change the way you see yourself? Why or why not?

_____

_____

_____

💻 **WWW *Activity:*** - Find more personality tests at the following websites:

- *http://www.emode.com*
- *http://www.outofservice.com/bigfive/*
- *http://www.colorquiz.com/*

2. **Self-Inventory**

What are you strengths, skills, and talents? List at least three things you are good at below. Then, list five things that make you happy or things you enjoy doing.

My strengths and talents:

- _____
- _____
- _____

Things that make me happy:

- _____
- _____
- _____

Self-Inventory Questions:

Was it difficult to come up with this list? Why or why not?

_____
_____
_____

Was this exercise helpful (Yes or No)? Explain.

_____
_____
_____

Did you find that some of the things that you were good at were also activities you enjoyed? What does that tell you?

_____
_____
_____

3. Personal Mission Statement

Develop your personal mission statement. Use the techniques from this section to draft your first mission statement. Use the lines below for your first draft. Remember--it can be as short or as long as you want it to be.

_____

_____

_____

_____

_____

_____

_____

_____

a. Read your mission statement. Does it give the reader an idea about your past, present and future? Does it give the reader an idea of how you want to live your life? Does it give clues about your personality, values, and accomplishments? If not, you may want to go back and rewrite your mission statement.

b. Have a friend or family member read your mission statement. What was their reaction? Now have someone you just met read it. How did they react to your mission statement? Ask them, based on your mission statement, what would they say if they were asked who you are by someone else.

c. What did you learn by writing your mission statement?

_____

_____

_____

d. Were you surprised by other people's reactions to it? Why or why not?

_____

_____

_____

CHAPTER 2 PROJECTS

1. Family Tree

Learning about your family will give you better insight into who you are and where you come from. Try to complete your own family tree. Interview your parents, grandparents, and other family members to find out your family history. Use the format below as a guide. Your family tree may be more complicated than this model.

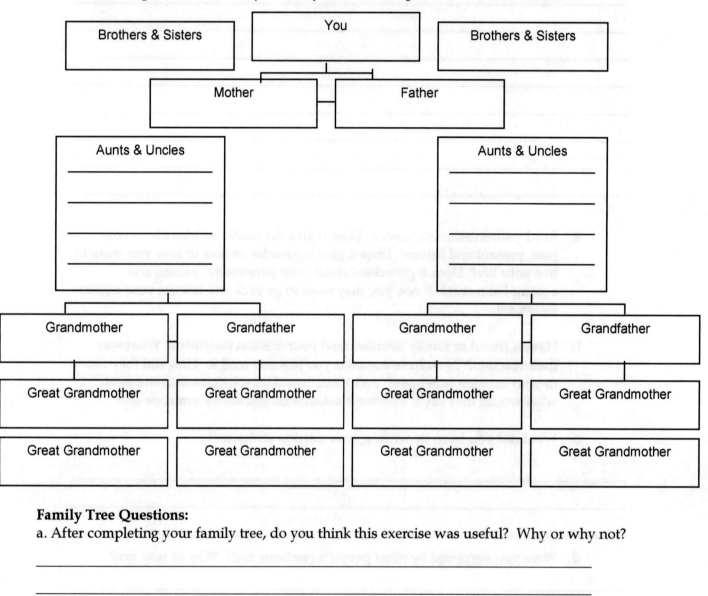

Family Tree Questions:

a. After completing your family tree, do you think this exercise was useful? Why or why not?

_____

_____

_____

b. Did you find out anything surprising about your family?

_____

_____

_____

2. My Goals

Refer to Activity 2 in the Introduction to Leadership Development section. What are the three leadership qualities you want to develop? Use what you learned about goal setting to write down your steps to developing one of those qualities. Refer to the sample on page 31.

Personal Leadership Plan: Part I

Goal: _____

_____

_____

What has stopped me from accomplishing this goal?

_____

_____

Objectives - *What do I have to do in order to meet my overall goal?*

- _____

- _____

- _____

Action Items - *What steps will I take to fulfill my short-term goals?*

- _____

- _____

- _____

Outcomes - *What happened as a result of your action plan?*

- _____

- _____

- _____

Evaluation - *Did I meet my goal? How can I improve my approach in the future?*

_____

_____

Copyright © 2001 New Light Leadership Coalition, Inc.   All Rights Reserved

SUGGESTED READING FOR CHAPTER 2

1. <u>Know Thyself</u> by Na'im Akbar

2. <u>From the Browder File: 22 Essays on the African American Experience</u> by Anthony T. Browder

3. <u>Black Roots: The Beginner's Guide to Tracing the African-American Family Tree</u> by Tony Burroughs

4. <u>Self Improvement: The Basis for Community Development</u> by the Honorable Minister Louis Farrakhan

5. <u>The Souls of Black Folk</u> by W.E.B. DuBois

6. <u>One Day My Soul Just Opened Up : 40 Days and 40 Nights Towards Spiritual Strength and Personal Growth</u> by Iyanla Vanzant

CHAPTER 3:
SOCIAL DEVELOPMENT

TOPICS IN SOCIAL DEVELOPMENT

- Environment & Culture
- Communication
- Team Building
- Conflict Resolution
- Public Speaking
- Social Responsibility

CHAPTER 3: SOCIAL DEVELOPMENT

Key Terms for Social Development

1. **ATONEMENT** reparation for a wrong or injury; amends

2. **COMMUNICATION** the imparting or interchange of thoughts, opinions, or information by speech, writing, or signs

3. **COMMUNITY** a group sharing common characteristics or interests and perceived or perceiving itself as distinct in some respect from the larger society within which it exists

4. **CONFLICT** to come into collision or disagreement; be contradictory, at variance, or in opposition; clash:

5. **CULTURE** the behaviors and beliefs characteristic of a particular social, ethnic, or age group

6. **ENVIRONMENT** 1. the social and cultural forces that shape the life of a person or a population 2. the aggregate of surrounding things, conditions, or influences; surroundings

7. **FAMILY** a group of persons sharing common ancestry, goals, or values

8. **GROUP** a number of persons considered together as being related in some way

9. **NETWORKING** a supportive system of sharing information and services among individuals and groups having a common interest

10. **PEER** a person who is equal to another in abilities, qualifications, age, background, and social status

11. **RELATIONSHIP** a connection, association, or involvement (between people)

12. **SOCIAL** of or pertaining to the life, welfare, and relations of human beings in a community

13. **SPEECH** ability to express one's thoughts and emotions by speech sounds and gestures

14. **STEREOTYPE** an oversimplified opinion, prejudiced attitude, or uncritical judgment

ENVIRONMENT & CULTURE

The term **social** refers to anything pertaining to the life, welfare, and relations of human beings in a **community**. In social development, we will explore the many influences our environment can have on us in shaping our lives.

ENVIRONMENT

Your **environment** consists of the social and cultural forces that shape your life. This includes everything in your surroundings—things, conditions, and other external influences. Your home, neighborhood, school, and even music are all things that shape the environment you live in.

Environments constantly change as you go throughout your life, and you pass through a variety of situations in just one day. In order to be successful, leaders must learn to master their environments and become a force of change within them instead of allowing the environment or circumstances to influence them.

We all create our own reality and have the ability to influence the world around us. If you were to walk into a library and suddenly scream "Fire!" you would drastically change the environment from calm and relaxing to one filled with chaos and confusion.

So how do we use this power in a positive way? It is simple. First, it is important for us to identify the external influences that allow us to make decisions and perform actions we otherwise would not. Here are some examples of external influences:

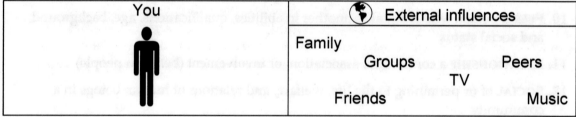

Figure 3.1: My Environment

In a survey from the New Light Leadership Coalition website, we asked what the number one influence is on young people today. Seventy of those surveyed agreed that most youth are greatly affected by their **peer** group more than **family**, television, music, and other external influences.

Do you agree that peers are most influential on the decisions you make? Explain.

_____

_____

_____

Copyright © 2001 New Light Leadership Coalition, Inc.   *All Rights Reserved*

CULTURE

Culture refers to the behaviors and beliefs characteristic of a particular social, ethnic, or age group. This includes everything from speech, dress, and any traditions relevant to a particular **group**. Think about your city, school, organization, or even your small circle of friends. There are things that are unique to each of these groups that projects a different cultural identity. If you belong to a sorority or fraternity, you go through a process of initiation that is unique to your organization. The sense of brotherhood or sisterhood is cultivated out of these traditions and rituals that are a part of the culture. Certain standards of behavior and a way of doing things are reinforced through culture.

Questions for Reflection & Discussion

What cultures do you belong to?

Do the groups you belong to define who you are?

What are the benefits of understanding your culture?

STEREOTYPES

A **stereotype** is a preconceived notion we have about another person based on their age, gender, class, or culture. When we stereotype others, we make assumptions about their background, character, and way of life.

While stereotypes usually have a negative connotation, it is important to understand that we can even stereotype a group of people with a positive or favorable trait. For instance, it is a stereotype in America that all Black people can dance. If you are Black and cannot dance, you may feel you have to fit into that stereotype because other people expect that from you.

Whether positive or negative, stereotypes usually have an adverse effect on **communication**. While it is important to be knowledgeable about other cultures, do not make assumptions about another human being until you learn something about them. Give them the chance to prove or disprove your perception of who they are through their own words, deeds, and actions. Everyone is part of a group of some sort but individuals have their own personalities and tastes, so be careful about judging others. Open, honest communication can combat many of the problems that arise when we stereotype.

POETRY AS AN EXPRESSION OF CULTURE

All civilizations leave something behind to give an indication of their culture. One of the most common ways we reveal things about our culture is through the written and spoken word. Poetry is a common tool used in communicating the culture of a particular group to others in a very intimate way. Poetry is usually written from the point of view of one member of a group and gives insight into the personal experience

---

Copyright © 2001 New Light Leadership Coalition, Inc. All Rights Reserved

involved in belonging to a particular cultural group. Read the following poem and look for clues into the culture of the author.

My Tomorrow Came Today	By Rodney Coates

Like Joseph and Daniel,
a master of your gate,
I became controller of my fate.

Fools disdain wisdom, choosing other fools
as companions and friends.
Books both instruct and confuse,
or simply fill spaces to collect dust.

From Diop to Franklin, James to Rodney,
Litwak to Hillard, Anderson to Woodson,
Chinweizu to Williams, Douglas to Du Bois,
Flying high with King and Akbar, Stamp and
Bell.

I learned differences between
dictation and revelation,
puff and stuff,
imagination and information.

Thus the beginning of wisdom was at hand.
Ignoring both stupid and dumb
choosing righteousness and truthfulness,
I came into the knowledge of self,
life, and all else.

Devotion to truth produces much sweet fruit,
whereas the fruit of folly is very bitter.

Lies, masquerading as truth, feels good but
erodes the soul and produces nothing.
Critical learning makes the difference.

Finding the spaces between Slavery and
freedom,

The paths toward success I traveled
Being blessed, much is now expected.

Ten things have I learned, I now depart to you:

All that is written is not true,
All that is true is not written.

What is called wisdom to some
is folly to many.
To many, the wise are considered to be fools,
and the fools are considered to be wise.

Self-hatred, often masquerading as conceit, is
really deceit and aims to defeat all others.

Ignorance, often masquerading as intelligence,
is really deception whose end is only
destruction.

Pride and boasting, like whiskey and drugs,
Leaves one hungover and disgusting.

Knowledge for knowledge sake, truth for the
sake of truth, and life for life. Stupidity is its
own reward.

Wisdom, beginning with humility, ends with
humility.

And my tomorrow came today.

Your Response to *My Tomorrow Came Today*

1. What did you learn about the culture of the author by reading this poem?

_____

_____

2. What cultural group do you think the author belongs to?

_____

3. What lines in the poem led you to make this assumption?

_____

_____

4. Could you identify with or relate to the poem? Why or why not?

_____

_____

COMMUNICATION

Communication refers to the imparting or interchange of thoughts, opinions, or information by speech, writing, signs, or symbols. Communication is a *process* involving a several components:

- *Sender* – gives message
- *Receiver* – gives meaning to the message
- *Channel* – medium used to convey the message
- *Sensory Channels* – your five senses
- *Message* – conveying an idea
- *Feedback* – receiver's interpretation and message back to sender
- *Situation* – overall setting [*i.e. place, relationship, etc.]*

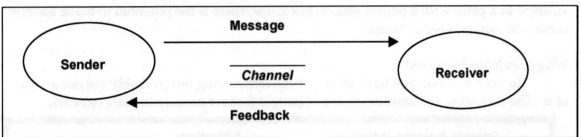

Figure 3.2: The Communication Process

TYPES OF COMMUNICATION

Intrapersonal – *within self*
Interpersonal – *between you and another person*
Group or Team – *between you and two or more people*
Public – *conveying a message to a large group*
Mass Media – *messages conveyed to a very large group of people using technology*

There are five basic types of communication. Intrapersonal communication involves thoughts within oneself. Interpersonal communication is between you and another individual. When communication with two or more others, you are participating in group or team communication. Public communication is the transmission of a message to a large group of people. The most common type of public communication is public speaking. This is a less personal type of communication. Finally, mass media involves radio, television, the Internet, and any other means used to transfer messages over a fairly large area to many different people.

Leaders must be good communicators. It is important to know what is appropriate for different situations. When speaking in public, for example, you may want to exemplify your best speaking while you may be more relaxed around a group of your peers. Knowing when to say what and how to say it will help you a great deal in relating with others.

NETWORKING

Networking is defined as a supportive system of sharing information and services among individuals and groups having a common interest. More simply, your personal network is made up of virtually everyone you have ever met. **Networking is being outgoing and meeting new people.**

Most people have heard that getting a job is not about what you know, but <u>who</u> you know. More than just a way to boost your career, networking will open your eyes to new experiences by meeting people you can learn from. You must use your network, but not in a selfish way. You should have a pool of individuals you can call on for advice and guidance, and they should also be able to call on for you. Each time you find yourself in a place with a person you do not know, there is the potential to make another contact to expand your network.

Who is in Your Network?
Believe it or not, you have already been networking but probably are not aware of it. The following are some examples of people that are already in your network.

> - Friends & Family Members
> - Classmates
> - Business Associates - *People you meet on the job*
> - Affiliations - *People you meet when you join clubs and organizations.*
> - Professors & Teachers
> - Internet Contacts

Figure 3.3: Your Network

Expanding Your Network
It can be intimidating to meet people for the first time, but everyone has a first introduction. Oftentimes, both people are nervous when they first meet. Break the ice by asking a question. If you get a one-word answer, keep asking questions. **People love to talk about themselves**. When you talk you learn nothing, but when you listen you learn about the other person and can pick out things about them you relate to. The person you meet at a social could be your future employer, business partner, or friend.

Professors can be good contacts to use as references on your resume. Develop a relationship with your professor by visiting his or her office to put a face to your name and social security number. This will expand your network and may even help your grade. Another way to get more contacts is to join a new organization or club and <u>be active</u>. Refrain from joining too many organizations just to beef up your resume. Spend quality time with the organizations you are in by being active on committees and attending meetings. In this age of information, the Internet is a good way to make new contacts. Be careful when trying to expand your online network--chat rooms are not a good way to meet people and there is no guarantee they are who they say they are. Instead, use email to make professional contacts with people from companies and organizations to which you are a member.

Travel often and invest in business cards for yourself. If you are still in school, get some business cards that indicate your major and name of your school. Printing is cheap and you can even make business cards with your own printer. Also, when you receive a business card from a new contact, write a note on the back to remind yourself who you met and what you talked about. It is best to do this after your conversation while it is fresh on your mind, but not while the person is talking to you. Be sure you stay in contact with everyone you meet. Do this by following up with a letter, card, or email that simply states you enjoyed meeting them. Every holiday, send the members of your network cards to remind them you exist. You would be surprised how effective this is in maintaining lines of communication with a person over the years.

LISTENING

Oftentimes, the most crucial part of communication is not fully practiced--listening. Listening shows the other person that you value their time and effort to communicate with you. As simple as it may sound, many things hinder us from listening to another person properly. Some examples are distractions, biases, disinterest, stereotypes, and even your own thoughts. Listening is the most important part of communication. Try to use some of the following techniques to show the sender that you understand the message.

ACTIVE LISTENING TECHNIQUES

Type of Statement	Purpose	Tips	Examples
Restate	To show that you understand and that you are listening.	Emphasize key facts and repeat the basic ideas.	"In other words, you . . ." "So you're saying. . ."
Reflect	To let others know you understand how they feel.	Repeat the basic feelings expressed.	"You're angry because . . ." "You feel . . ."
Encourage	To show interest and keep the person talking.	Use a positive tone of voice and do not agree or disagree.	"That's interesting" "Mmm hmm" "I see"
Summarize	To review main points and encourage further discussion.	Restate and reflect main facts and feelings.	"If I understand you correctly, . . ."

Figure 3.4: Active Listening Techniques

NONVERBAL COMMUNICATION

Nonverbal communication includes facial expressions, tones of voice, gestures, eye contact, touch, and movement. More powerful than verbal communication, nonverbal communication gives better insight into the motivations of the sender of a message. What you do is more important that what you say. Body language is important because it can reinforce verbal communication. It also can show mixed meanings. For example, if a man if giving a speech about how excited he is about a new project, but his tone of voice is low, he is slouching, and his eyes are focused on the floor instead of the audience, you may not believe him. You can use your body language to support or contradict your words.

Nonverbal messages communicate emotion, are seen are more reliable, and also can have a cultural context. The problem with nonverbal communication, as with any form of expression, is that it can be interpreted inaccurately by the receiver of the message. The same man who slouched while giving a speech about his exciting new project may really be excited about his subject but is very shy in front of a large group of people. Another example of misinterpretation of nonverbal messages relating to culture involved hand gestures. In the United States, if you raise your middle finger at a person they would be quite offended. If the same person went to Russia and wanted to show their anger with another person, they may try to use the same gesture only it will not have the same effect. In Russia, raising your middle finger means nothing, but raising your ring finger may offend someone even if that was not your intention.

TEAM BUILDING

It is essential for leaders to be able to communicate with others—especially in small groups or teams. A group is a number of persons considered together as being related in some way. Businesses and organizations are made up of groups that work together to accomplish a goal.

GROUP DYNAMICS

Groups go through several different stages. As a leader, it is important to understand which stage your group is in and take the necessary steps to move the group to the next level.

Stages of Group Development
Generally, there are five steps involved in the development of a group. They are forming, storming, norming, performing, and adjourning.

Stage 1: Forming
During the forming stage, groups are trying to adjust to their new role. Group members are dependent on routine behaviors and look to the group leader for direction. Heavy topics are avoided in an attempt to keep things simple during this beginning stage. Members are trying to become oriented to their functions in the group as well as getting to know one another. To grow to the next stage, members must move out of the comfort zone of conflict-free interaction.

Stage 2: Storming
In the storming phase, conflict and competition arise along with organization. As the group members attempt to organize to accomplish their purpose, conflict inevitably results in their personal relations. Individuals have to learn to set-aside personality differences to accomplish the goal of the group. In order to move to stage three, group members should listen more and focus on problem solving instead of personalities.

Stage 3: Norming
In the norming stage, the group starts to balance out. Members learn to get along and are focused on the tasks of the group. There is a shared sense of leadership and members identify with each other better. A sense of belonging among group members grows in this stage. Creativity is high and information and ideas are shared freely. The norming stage can make the group members sensitive to change as they get used to how they function together.

Stage 4: Performing
This stage, which many groups do not get to, is interdependence. In this stage, people can work independently, in smaller groups, or as a unit without any member feeling dependent or inadequate. Leadership roles adjust to the needs of the group. This stage is the most productive and members are confident in performing tasks without needed assurance from other group members. There is unity and the group is loyal. Everyone is focused on the success of the group.

Stage 5: Adjourning

The adjourning stage is when group functions and **relationships** dissolve. If a project ends or the group is no longer needed, members leave the group and go their separate ways.

THE TEAM LEADER

Without team leadership, teams will be ineffective. Team leadership is different than traditional types of leadership. Control over the final decision is not held by the leader but is left to the group. The importance of one's position and power are de-emphasized in team leadership. The team leader should see the group not as individuals but as a collective. The task-oriented functions of the team are not performed only by the leader but are shared by the entire group.

> **DUTIES OF THE TEAM LEADER**
> - Keeps the team on task
> - Initiates team activities
> - Maintains all team roles & responsibilities
> - Guides without dominating
> - Involves all members
> - Sticks to agenda, process
> - Helps group reach consensus

A team leader's duties involve being a facilitator and reminding group members of the task at hand. Team leaders guide the group through decision-making processes and encourage the involvement of all members. Each member of a team is equally important and contributes to the team.

Guidelines for Building a Team

Teams must be small enough in the number of members and each member must possess an adequate skill level that complements other team members. The purpose of the team must be meaningful and clearly defined goals and objectives should be in place.

TEAM EFFECTIVENESS

Members must have a sense of mutual accountability. The entire group, not just the team leader, shares responsibility for group effectiveness. The closeness of a team environment allows the team leader to identify the members' needs and issues more easily. Expressing feelings about the effectiveness of the team should not be discouraged, but rather encouraged by team leaders. Issues should be addressed and dealt with openly in meetings to prevent small problems from becoming big ones.

> **SIGNS OF AN INEFFECTIVE TEAM**
> - NON-PRODUCTIVE ARGUMENTS
> - TOO MUCH AGREEMENT
> - NOT DELIVERING RESULTS
> - LACK OF INTEREST OR MOTIVATION

TEAM BUILDING ACTIVITIES

Team building activities are used to promote togetherness among team members. They should promote the development of skills necessary for team development. Strategic planning and conflict resolution exercises are common team building activities.

Below are a few suggestions for team building activities:

Leadership Retreat
The purpose of a leadership retreat is to build bonds between the members of a group and develop an agenda for future activities to be planned by the group. Retreats are also used to resolve any conflicts that need to be addressed in an environment unfamiliar to the group members. The best thing about a retreat is the chance to spend the weekend, at no cost, in an environment that is not experienced everyday. Suggestions for planning a successful leadership retreat can be found in the *NLLC Youth Leaders Roundtable Agenda.*

The Blind Leading the Blind
This activity can be performed at a leadership retreat or executive board meeting. The team members are tied together at the ankles. The team leader is asked to lead the group through a maze. The catch is the team leader is blindfolded. The team leader has to rely on the team members to direct him or her through the maze. Creating boundaries with rope, chairs, tables or anything else that can be used to make a clear path can serve as a maze. If anyone in the group, including the team leader, steps on or bumps into one of the boundaries they are disqualified. To make it more competitive, set a time limit to get through the maze.

Outdoor Experience
A camping trip is an ideal opportunity for team building. This isolates members of the team to a different and unfamiliar environment and forces them to rely on each other for basic needs. A camping trip can build relationships between team members that ordinarily may not get to know each other outside of a business-like environment (meetings, organizational projects, etc.). It also challenges team members physically as well as mentally. Team members will learn to cooperate with each other and deal with the strengths and weaknesses of team members.

CONFLICT RESOLUTION

In order to work well with other people, leaders must be good at resolving conflict.

 A **conflict** is a situation causing disunity or discord between two individuals or groups.

Conflicts are usually caused by a perceived feeling of hurt, insult, or injury.

To resolve a conflict, it is important to *rise above emotion*.

Use the following steps to approach solving conflicts with others peacefully:

STEPS TO SOLVING A CONFLICT

1. ADOPT A PEACEFUL ATTITUDE

You should never be the aggressor or the cause of a conflict. Try to avoid physical confrontations if possible.

2. LISTEN, LISTEN, LISTEN

The main problem during a conflict is that both parties want to get their point across. This causes them to want to speak before the other person is heard. It is important to LISTEN in order to resolve a conflict.

3. STATE YOUR DESIRE TO WORK THINGS OUT

*The other party must know that you are willing to **compromise**. A compromise is the process of give and take that leads to a middle ground where BOTH PARTIES are content.*

4. BE A MODEL OF SUPPORT & COOPERATION

Be sincere in your attempt to reconcile with another party.

GUIDELINES TO RESOLVING CONFLICT

☑ **Never** approach an individual in front of friends or a group, this will only cause them to defend themselves. They will retaliate instead of cooperating with you.

☑ **Do not insult** the other party. Tell him or her what they are doing that is hurting you and ask them to stop.

☑ **Do not provoke** the other person or group. This will only lead to further conflict and possibly violence.

☑ **Be calm!** Instead of approaching the situation emotionally, give yourself a moment to cool down before trying to deal with the conflict. Emotion can cause unnecessary confusion and the root of the problem will never be discovered or solved.

Figure 3.5: Conflict Management Tips

CONFLICT MANAGEMENT SUGGESTIONS

1. Have the team identify the criteria they will use to make decisions and evaluate the conflicting ideas against each criterion.

2. Have participants silently post their ideas on the board and write the pros and cons of each suggestion.

3. When two people disagree, ask each to reflect the opposite position until the other person's position is fully understood.

4. Summarize the issues on which there is agreement and confirm to show progress and possibilities.

5. Look for non-verbal signs of dissent and address them openly.

6. Never take sides. Instead, suggest a way for the team to overcome its roadblock.

THE 8 STEPS OF ATONEMENT

Atonement is a process making amends for a fault or wrongdoing. In order to resolve our problems with one another, we must follow these steps:

1. **Point Out Wrong or Fault** – *Let it be known that a wrong was committed.*

2. **Acknowledge the Wrong** – *No matter who brings it to your attention, admit that you were at fault.*

3. **Confession** – *Confess to your Creator and the person whom you wronged.*

4. **Repentance** – *Show remorse for your actions and sincerely promising to change.*

5. **Atonement** – *Do something to make up for your actions.*

6. **Forgiveness** – *Seeking forgiveness from the individual wronged and your Creator, and forgiving yourself for your transgressions.*

7. **Reconciliation** – *To settle differences and make peace with self and those whom you have wronged.*

8. **Perfect Union** – *Oneness with your Creator, family, and friends*

PUBLIC SPEAKING

If you have not already had to speak in front of a group of people, you will be called upon to do so someday. Even if you do not wish to be in the spotlight, college courses and the jobs you choose will force you to conquer the fear most people have of public speaking.

ORGANIZING A SPEECH

There are three basic reasons for speaking: to inform, to persuade, or to entertain. Most speeches are organized with the opening or attention grabber, subject, and conclusion. Your opening should catch the audience's attention and get them interested in what you plan to discuss.

Establishing credibility is also important when delivering a **speech**. If you are talking to a group of parents about effective parenting techniques and you have no children, they probably will not take you seriously. You should qualify yourself by saying that you have no experience as a parent but you have been a child and can speak from that perspective.

For younger speakers, it is important to establish credibility so adults will take you seriously. Sometimes, an older audience will think of you are more of a novelty or "cute" unless you establish your credibility with them. When speaking, you should choose at least three clear points to discuss. Organize your speech well in the same manner you would an essay. Keep the audience interested and conclude with something memorable. If you are speaking to persuade, include a call to action. What are you persuading the audience to do?

1) **Opening or Attention Grabber** - *Leads into subject of speech.*
   a) Question
   b) Joke
   c) Story
   d) Interesting Fact or Statistic

2) **Establish Credibility** - *Tell the audience why you are qualified to speak on the subject*

3) **Subject Matter** -*Talk about your topic*
   a) Organize speech into subtopics
   b) Use supporting facts to give evidence of your argument

4) **Conclusion** - *Leave the audience with something positive or memorable.*
   a) Persuasive speech: Appeal to action.
   b) Review
   c) Memorable Statement

SEVEN STEPS TO PREPARING A SPEECH

1 - Select a Topic – Pick a topic appropriate for your audience.

2 - Determine the Purpose – What is your purpose? Is it to inform, persuade, or entertain?

3 - Analyze the Audience and the Occasion –
Audience: What do they know about the topic? What interest do they have in the topic? What is their attitude towards your chosen topic?
Occasion – What is the reason for the deliverance of the speech?

4 - Find Material – Is it something you already know about? Is it something that you have to research? Do you need to interview anyone?

5 - Word the Speech – Prepare an outline and then fill in the outline. Try to follow one train of thought. DO NOT WRITE THE ENTIRE SPEECH. The worst presentation is one that is scripted and read to your audience. Use your outline as a guideline and know what you want to talk about.

6 - Practice the Delivery – Practice the speech in the mirror or in front of friends. Try to memorize your main points but not the entire speech. Memorization makes the speech sound rehearsed and forced. You want to be able to sound as though you are having a conversation with the audience.

7 - Deliver the Speech – The most important thing to remember when delivering a speech is to stay focused. If you go off on a tangent, refer back to your outline to keep you on track. If you are nervous speaking in front of people, be comforted by knowing that most great speakers feel nervous before addressing a crowd.

Once you conquer the fear of speaking in public, it will become easier and you will be more comfortable expressing yourself and giving presentations. Eventually you will develop your own style of speech. Remember to keep practicing because you never know when you will be called on to speak.

SOCIAL RESPONSIBILITY

Leaders must adopt social responsibility. Social responsibility involves taking action in your community. Volunteering and community service are vital aspects of leadership. Your perspective on the world around you will change as you learn that others are less fortunate than you are. Helping others is a fulfilling activity that allows you to give of yourself to others. Community service shows that you are grateful for the many things that you have and are willing to share with others.

It is easy to volunteer, and there are many programs that you can choose to be involved in. The places most in need of volunteers are probably your local hospitals and nursing homes. It's as easy as calling the information desk at the appropriate institution and asking to speak to the volunteer coordinator. I guarantee you won't be turned down!

When you volunteer at a hospital, you'll probably work at the gift shop or information desk, distribute food and drinks to patients, or simply keep patients company. The time commitment is usually minimal and you can often set your own schedule. Any way you do it, nothing is more rewarding than a smile on someone else's face whose day you just brightened!

Every organization should have a community service component. Community service is another good way for members to bond with each other while helping others. Planning a community service project is easy--it just requires a few phone calls and people who are dedicated to give up a few hours of their time out of a week. Your members could organize a tutoring program at a local school or organize a blood drive with the Red Cross on your campus.

Below are some resources you can use to plan a community service project.

FIND VOLUNTEERING OPPORTUNITIES IN YOUR COMMUNITY

http://www.servenet.org - home of Youth Service America. Site includes daily service news, online resources and volunteer opportunity postings, searchable by zip code.

http://www.grass-roots.org -- tells the stories of the most innovative grassroots programs in the United States and the local heroes who've found effective ways to build their communities, fix what's broken and make them better.

http://www.idealist.org -- includes a directory of thousands of nonprofit websites, an online library for nonprofits and a database of volunteer opportunities nationwide.

http://www.communityservice.org -- searchable index of volunteer opportunities.

CHAPTER 3 REVIEW QUESTIONS

1. What is a group? Name and describe one step of the group formation process.

_____

_____

_____

2. a. Define "culture."

_____

_____

_____

    b. What symbols identify your culture?

_____

_____

_____

3. What is the most important part of communication? Why?

_____

_____

_____

4. What is the best way to resolve a conflict?

_____

_____

_____

Copyright © 2001 New Light Leadership Coalition, Inc.   *All Rights Reserved*

CHAPTER 3 ACTIVITIES

1. **Group Dynamics**. Observe a group and identify the leader.

Group Leader_____

- How did you know this person was the leader?

_____

_____

_____

_____

- Was the leader a positive or negative effect on the group?

_____

_____

_____

_____

2. **Stereotypes**: List some common stereotypes about males and females below and answer the questions. Some examples are females are too emotional and all males strong.

Female Stereotypes	Male Stereotypes
_____	_____
_____	_____
_____	_____
_____	_____
_____	_____

a. How do these stereotypes effect the way you view and interact with the opposite sex?

_____

_____

_____

b. How do these perceptions effect the way you view yourself and your capabilities?

_____

_____

_____

c. How can you prevent yourself from falling victim to using these stereotypes when judging other people?

_____

_____

_____

3. Describe a conflict you have been involved in recently.

_____

_____

_____

◆ How did you handle the situation?

_____

_____

_____

◆ How could you have handled it better?

_____

_____

_____

CHAPTER 3 PROJECTS

1. **Speech.** Write a speech on the topic of your choice. If you cannot think of a topic, try to write a speech about why leadership development is important for young people to learn. Refer to the *Seven Steps for Speech Preparation* for guidelines. Practice delivering your speech in front of family or friends.

• Were you nervous when delivering you speech? YES NO SOMEWHAT

• Do you feel more comfortable with your speech skills? Why or why not?

_____

_____

_____

2. **Conflict Management**

Do you get into conflicts often? ____yes ____no ____sometimes

Use the goal setting model from Chapter 2 to write a plan for developing your conflict management skills if you need improvement in this area. Start by answering the questions below:

- What is the root of most of your conflicts with others?

_____

_____

_____

_____

- How can you improve your behavior to prevent them?

_____

_____

_____

_____

3. Personal Leadership Plan: Part II

What are your goals for social development? After reading this chapter, pick something you would like to work on as it relates to your social development. Do you want to work on your networking skills, become a better listener, or polish your public speaking style? Refer back to the sample on page 31 to help with this project.

Personal Leadership Plan: Part II

Social Development Goal(s): _____

_____

_____

_____

What has stopped me from accomplishing this goal?

_____

_____

Objectives - *What do I have to do in order to meet my overall goal?*

- _____

- _____

- _____

Action Items - *What steps will I take to fulfill my objectives?*

-

- _____
- _____

Outcomes - *What happened as a result of your action plan?*

- _____
- _____
- _____

Evaluation - *Did I meet my goal? How can I improve my approach in the future?*

_____

_____

4. **Community Service.** Volunteer at your local hospital, nursing home, or another institution for at least one month. Commit to volunteering at least once a week during the month of your choice. Keep track of your volunteering hours in the following table:

OR

Organize a community service project for your organization. Use the following table to keep track of the volunteer hours for your members.

Volunteer Hours for the Month of _____

Example

Sunday	Monday	Tuesday	Wednesday	Thursday	Friday	Saturday
2 hours - Tutoring			2 hours - Tutoring			4 hours - Red Cross

Sunday	Monday	Tuesday	Wednesday	Thursday	Friday	Saturday

What did you learn from your volunteering experience?

_____

_____

_____

_____

Would you recommend that other young people volunteer? Why or why not?

_____

_____

_____

_____

SUGGESTED READING LIST FOR CHAPTER 3

1. The Isis Papers: Keys to the Colors by Dr. Frances Cress-Welsing

2. Team-Building Activities for Every Group by Alanna Jones

3. The Power of Positive Confrontation: The Skills You Need to Know to Handle Conflicts at Work, at Home, and in Life by Barbara Pachter

4. Worldwide Volunteering for Young People 2000 by Roger Potter

5. How to Win Friends and Influence People by Dale Carnegie

CHAPTER 4:
EDUCATIONAL DEVELOPMENT

TOPICS IN EDUCATIONAL DEVELOPMENT

- Education
- Learning Styles
- Getting into College
- Career Planning

Key Terms for Educational Development

1. **ACADEMIC** 1. a narrow focus on or display of learning 2. hypothetical or theoretical and not expected to produce an immediate or practical result

2. **ACHIEVE** to gain with effort

3. **ACHIEVEMENT** the act of accomplishing something

4. **APTITUDE** capability; ability; innate or acquired capacity for something

5. **EDUCATION** 1. knowledge acquired by learning and instruction 2. the act or process of imparting or acquiring general knowledge, developing the powers of reasoning and judgment, and generally of preparing oneself or others intellectually for mature life

6. **INFORMATION** knowledge gained through study, communication, research, instruction

7. **LEARN** to acquire knowledge of or skill in by study, instruction, or experience

8. **KNOWLEDGE** 1. acquaintance with facts, truths, or principles 2. clear and certain mental apprehension.

9. **STUDY** consider in detail and subject to an analysis in order to discover essential features or meaning; examine

10. **TALENT** a capacity for achievement or success

11. **TEACHER** one who imparts knowledge or skill

12. **UNDERSTANDING** the state of perceiving and comprehending the nature and significance of

13. **WISDOM** understanding *and* acting on what is true, right, or lasting; insight

EDUCATION

Education is the sum total of everything we have learned throughout our lives. The amount of **knowledge, wisdom,** and **understanding** we accumulate in school and through life experience allows us to have a better understanding of the world we live in.

"The only thing that interferes with my learning is my education."

-Albert Einstein

Some people believe that our **academic** future is only based on what we learn in school. That could not be further from the truth. What we learn in school must be supplemented by real life experience in order to benefit us.

Ideally, education and the thirst for knowledge will allow us to advance our education and become well-rounded individuals. Our personal academic **achievement** will be based on the initiative we take to learn new things. No one else can give us our education, but once we have it, it is the one thing that cannot be taken away from us.

The difference between a person having knowledge and a person having knowledge but lacking understanding is simple. Knowledge simply means you know, understanding means that you know *why*. If you know that two plus four equals six, it is mere memorization unless you understand the mathematical concept behind the numbers 2 and 4. A person with knowledge does not necessarily change their actions based on what they know. However, one with understanding will show their knowledge through how they live their lives. A person who continues to act based on what they know and understand is called wise. This is why many elders have wisdom, because they have learned through years of experience in practicing what they know.

All of us are born with innate **talents**, or gifts that come easily to us. You may know someone who can play the piano very well but just started taking lessons. This person has an **aptitude** or capability to play music. However, if these gifts and talents are not harnessed through **study** and practice, we will soon lose all of our great abilities. If the same piano student does not continue to work on his or her skill and continue to take lessons, they will never master the art of playing the piano like Duke Ellington.

Sometimes, what we know can hinder us from wanting to **learn** more. If we feel that we are an expert on a particular subject, we will close our ears to other people who have new or different information we may not have heard. Education can cause you to become close minded if you allow it to. The key to education is always having a desire to learn more. If you open up your mind to new ideas and critically evaluate information, you will continue on the journey of education and academic achievement for your entire life.

LEARNING STYLES

Have you ever wondered why sometimes you just don't understand a concept in class, no matter how many times the **teacher** explains it? Or, why some things are so easy for you to understand while others are puzzled? It could be because of your particular style of learning.

All of us have different ways that we learn. Some people enjoy reading a book while others would prefer to watch a movie. The key to getting the most out of your education is being able to understand your learning style and adjusting your study habits to meet your needs. The three major types of learners are *visual*, *auditory*, and *kinesthetic*.

TYPES OF LEARNING STYLES

👁**Visual learners** learn better when they are able to see what is being taught. For example, a visual learner may prefer to see a pie chart describing information about the number of students in their class who received an 'A' on the last test as opposed to the teacher reading numbers to them.

👂 **Auditory learners** retain information more efficiently when they hear things. An auditory learner may do well on a test after listening to a lecture, whereas just reading a textbook may not enable him or her to grasp all of the information on a subject.

✋**Kinesthetic Learners** enjoy learning when they are involved in hands-on activities. After listening to the teacher explain how chemicals react when mixed together, the kinesthetic learner will understand the concept better after the class performs a lab experiment.

What is Your Learning Style?

You may already know what your learning style is by reading the above descriptions. There are also tests that can help you discover your personal learning style. One you understand how you learn, you can improve your study habits and will be able to retain more of the information you are taught.

Complete Activity 1 at the end of this chapter before continuing to the next page.

STUDY TIPS FOR YOUR LEARNING STYLE

Below is a brief description of the different learning styles and some techniques you can use to help you study and learn better.

Visual Learners Usually:	Visual Learners Should:
• Need to see it to know it. • Have strong sense of color. • May have artistic ability. • Often have difficulty with spoken directions. • May over-react to sounds. • May have trouble following lectures. • Often misinterprets words.	• Use graphics to reinforce learning; films, slides, illustrations, & diagrams. • Color-code to organize notes and possessions. • Ask for written directions. • Use flow-charts and diagrams for note taking. • Visualize spelling of words or facts in order to memorize them.
Auditory Learners Usually: • Prefer to get information by listening • Need to hear it to know it. • May have difficulty following written directions. • Difficulty with reading. • Problems with writing. • Inability to read body language and facial expressions.	**Auditory Learner Should:** • Use tapes for reading and for class and lecture notes. • Learn by interviewing or by participating in discussions. • Have test questions or directions read aloud or put on tape.
Kinesthetic Learners Usually: • Prefer hands-on learning. • Can assemble parts without reading directions. • Have difficulty sitting still. • Learn better when physical activity is involved. • May be very well coordinated and have athletic ability.	**Kinesthetic Learners Should:** • Engage in experiential learning (making models, doing lab work, and role-playing). • Take frequent breaks in study periods. • Trace letters and words to learn spelling and remember facts. • Use a computer to reinforce learning through sense of touch. • Memorize or drill while walking & exercising. • Express abilities through dance, drama or sports.

Adapted from the Tutor Trainer's Manual, Tyler Junior College, Tyler,TX.

Figure 4.1: Learning Style Study Tips

GETTING INTO COLLEGE

The school you decide to attend for college is one of the most important decisions you will have to make. First, you have to decide very early in your high school career that you want to attend college. You may have heard that your freshman year in high school is not significant and will not be considered by admissions officers. However, this is the first year you have to establish a solid grade point average (GPA). This is something that will follow you throughout your high school career and will count towards your cumulative grade point average (GPA).

CHOOSING A COLLEGE

You have several options when considering higher education. Many students do not feel comfortable going right into a four-year institution. There are two-year schools that offer certificate programs and community colleges that will allow you to get more practice with some subjects you may not have done as well as you would have liked to in high school.

When considering a college to attend, think about your own likes and dislikes. What is important to you in a college? You may want to brainstorm and come up with a list of qualities and characteristics you want your ideal college to have. Is living near home important to you? The field of study you choose may also influence your college choice. If you want to be a doctor, Johns Hopkins University or MIT may be better choices than your local state college.

COLLEGE CHARACTERISTICS TO CONSIDER						
Location		Majors/ Degrees Offered		Accredited Programs		
	Size		Urban, Rural, Suburban			Diversity
Average SAT Score		Reputation		Graduation/D rop-out Rate		
	Cost of Living		Tuition			Social Activities

A popular reason to choose a college may be that many of your friends will go to that school. While having friends on campus may help you adjust to campus life, especially if you move away from home, that may not be the best reason to settle on one institution over the other. A big part of your college experience is meeting new people and concentrating on what you plan to do with your professional career. A great deal of what you learn in college will take place outside of the classroom. Whatever you choose to do, you should continue your education throughout your life.

Copyright © 2001 New Light Leadership Coalition, Inc.   *All Rights Reserved*

APPLYING

Once you have decided on what schools you want to apply to you must fill out the applications. Some schools use general applications you can use to apply to more than one school. Pay attention to deadlines and make sure you take both the SAT and ACT tests. Give yourself enough time to take them more than once so you will have a better chance of getting a hire score. Many schools will also require you to submit an essay.

The Essay

The essay is often the most important part of the application because it gives the admissions officers a glimpse at the real you. Make sure you choose a topic that you can write freely about. If the college gives you several options, choose the topic that will allow you to highlight your best qualities and experiences.

Your essay should reveal things about your personal experience in and out of school. Even though it is a personal essay, treat it like a school paper. Make sure your grammar and spelling are flawless. You may even want your English teacher to review your essay for mistakes before submitting it to the college.

SCHOLARSHIPS & FINANCIAL AID

There are many options to consider when financing your college education. Before you start looking for money fill out your FAFSA form. The FAFSA is the federal student aid form that will determine your eligibility for some grants and scholarships. Some colleges use the FAFSA form to select students for institutional grants and scholarships. The FAFSA form is available in your school's financial aid or guidance office. You can also fill out the form online at http://www.fafsa.gov

Below are some options you have to finance your education.

Scholarships

Scholarships are awards granted by universities, private foundations, special interest groups, and other organizations. The best part about scholarships is that unlike student loans, they do not have to be repaid. Most scholarships do require you to maintain a certain grade point average.

You can apply for scholarships by consulting your school's guidance office. You can also find scholarships online at websites like Fastweb.com. Fastweb.com allows you to personalize your search for scholarships and will notify you when new scholarships that you quality for are announced. You can also find Scholarship guides at your local library.

Grants

The most common grant given by the United States government is the Pell Grant. Most grants are based on financial need rather than academic criteria. If your parents' income is upper-middle class to high-income many federal grants will be unavailable to you.

Student Loans

Most people do not want to take out student loans because of the enormous debt involved. Scholarships and grants should be your first avenues for financing your education. Student loans are a last resort but are also manageable. You will not have to pay back your loans until you graduate from school. Try to borrow only as much money as you need and keep your lifestyle in check while you are in school. Do not go on shopping sprees every week. Live within your means and pay attention to the date you will have to begin repaying your loan and the rate of interest. Do not make the minimum payment on your loan. It is always better to try to pay more than that to pay your loan of quicker and with less accumulated interest.

Fellowships

A fellowship is money granted by a university or foundation or other agency for advanced study or research. Fellowships are usually available for students interested in pursuing post-graduate education and are offered by private foundations and other institutions. There are fellowships for all areas of study. The requirements are similar to scholarships but require specialized study in most cases.

COLLEGE INTERVIEW

The schools you apply to may not require an interview, but it is always a good idea to request one if it is feasible. Giving recruiters a chance to meet you in person can make a difference in their decision to admit you to their school.

Refer to the interview tips in the Career Planning section for how to conduct yourself during an interview. Most of the same principles apply when getting ready for your college interview.

CAREER PLANNING

CAREER OPTIONS

What career will you go into when you finish school? The answer should be something you enjoy doing, but is may also depend upon the options available to you. For example, at the turn of the last century delivering milk to homes was a popular job but today, most people buy milk from the grocery store instead of a milkman.

What jobs are going to be popular in the next few years? According to the U.S. Department of Labor, the following jobs will grow at the fastest rate between now and 2006. As you can see, experts predict that the computer and health-care industries will provide many job opportunities.

Occupation	Percent Change Between 1999 and 2006
Database administrators/computer support specialists/other computer scientists	118
Computer engineers	109
Systems analysts	103
Personal and home-care aides	85
Physical- and corrective-therapy assistants and aides	79
Home-health aides	76
Medical assistants	74
Desktop-publishing specialists	74
Physical therapists	71
Occupational-therapy assistants and aides	69

Figure 4.2: Occupational Outlook 1999-2006

CHOOSING A CAREER

Choosing a career is one of the most important decisions you will make. When choosing a career, consider your strengths and weaknesses. You may want to consider some of the following questions while trying to decide on a career.

- What do you like to do?
    - Do you prefer working with people or keeping to yourself?
        - When do you want to retire?
            - How much money do you want to make?
                - What are your favorite subjects in school?
                    - What comes easily to you?
                        - Do you want to work 9 to 5?
                            - Is advancement important?

Copyright © 2001 New Light Leadership Coalition, Inc. *All Rights Reserved*

It may be best to write down three different careers or fields that strike your interest. Once you have charted out the pros and cons of your career choices, do some research. It is a good idea to shadow someone who works in the field you are interested in entering for a workday to get a feel for what you would actually be doing. Sometimes the ideal of a career is not what it turns out to be. For instance, if you want to be a mathematician because you like math, you may decide not to be a mathematician when you find out the limits of that field. Instead, you may consider engineering--which incorporates many mathematical concepts into practical solutions and has many more job opportunities.

Go to job and career fairs and talk to the company representatives. Ask them about their companies and what you can do in the field you are interested in. Inquire about what the requirements are for different jobs and what the need is for your field of interest. By doing this type of first-hand research, you will get a good idea of what the reality is in the job market of what you would like to do.

Now that you have decided on your career, it is time to look for your first job or internship. There are several things you want to consider before pursuing an employment opportunity. You should do your homework—that means researching the company you are interesting in working for and making sure you can handle the job. What kind of benefits do they offer? What is their company culture? Are there opportunities for advancement?

The first thing you need to do even before searching ads in newspapers or talking to on-campus recruiters is prepare a resume.

YOUR RESUME

Your resume is the first impression a potential employer will have of you. The purpose of preparing a resume is to get to the job interview. A poorly composed resume will make you look unprofessional and give the impression the job is not important to you.

If you use an online career service such as *JobDirect.com* or *Jobs.com*, you can create your own resume online fairly easily. However, it is still important to have several hard copies on hand.

In today's competitive job market, companies are deluged with resumes and cover letters for a finite number of openings. Typically, employers will spend only 15 to 20 seconds on each resume. The purpose of the resume is to get to the job interview.

Marketing Your Skills

Think of your resume as a sales tool. This is the first impression your potential employer will have of you. Your resume should not summarize your job responsibilities; rather it should focus on you accomplishments and contributions. It is important to remember your competition may have a similar work history or education. Emphasize your successes and unique strengths.

What Employers Look for in a Resume

Employers prefer one-page resumes. Do not overload them with useless information. If you are applying for an entry-level position at a sales firm, they may not be concerned with the three months you spent working at the local Baskin Robins. Your resume should appear neat and organized. Use a succinct style that quickly conveys your past performance and future capabilities. Never put your social security number, age, date of birth, or other unnecessary personal information on a resume.

Chronological Resume

The chronological resume is the most common resume format. This form is best for individuals with a solid work history and effective for people staying within the same field. It is also appropriate for recent college graduates and is preferred by most employers. When writing a chronological resume, you should list education first, follow education with relevant work experience, and include part-time and summer positions, volunteer work, and internships.

BUILDING A CHRONOLOGICAL RESUME

Header

The header must include your name, address and phone number. Work phone number, fax, and email address are optional.

Objective

Listing your objective is optional. If you know what you want to do with your career, then be sure to put your objective on your resume to let potential employers know what you want to do. If you are still researching potential career paths, then it might be best to leave an objective off your resume. Sometimes a narrow objective will cause employers to exclude you for a position you might want to try. Even if a job or internship is not exactly correlated with your major, it could still provide valuable work experience. Make sure you know what you want out of your job experience and communicate that clearly on your resume.

- Optional.
- Effective for showing interest in a particular field.
- Effective for entry-level applications.

Experience

Experience is the most crucial element of a chronological resume. Keep your statements brief and to the point and focus on your accomplishments. For college students and recent college graduates, you may not have that much important work experience. Do not put a job on your resume that you had for less than a year, unless it is all the work experience you have. Also, list your volunteer work and community service as experience. Even though you were not paid, valuable skills are gained by volunteering and employers do consider it when reviewing your resume.

Be sure to show quantitative or otherwise tangible results.

- Avoid use of the word "I".
- Use active verbs such as "Managed" or "Directed."
- Eliminate positions held for less than four months.
- Round off dates to years (1992-1993 instead of "6/92-3/93").

Education: Recent College Graduates
Emphasize your strengths:

* High GPA (3.0+).   * Awards and Honors.
* Relevant courses.   * Extracurricular activities.

Personal Information and References
Personal information is optional. Do not include references on resumes. Stating that "References are available upon request" is sufficient. Do not include any information about your race, marital status, age, weight, or religion.

Sample Resume

Marie Johnson
1234 Horizon Road
Strawberry, Ohio USA
(555) 555-5555
Marie.Johnson@nllc.zzn.com

Objective: To obtain a position as an elementary school teacher.

Education:

Anytown University - Anytown, USA   General University - Mytown, USA
B.S., Elementary Education, 1998-2000   Major: **Education**, 1997-1998 (GPA 3.52)

Experience:

Lincoln Elementary School - Mytown, MD   9/99- 5/00
Teaching Internship
- Gained invaluable experience as a student teacher in third and fourth grade classroom settings.
- Developed/implemented lesson plans, administered tests and evaluations, and analyzed student performance.
- Conducted group/individual reading, math and art activities.
- Provided personalized training and tutoring assistance and ministered to children with special needs.
- Fostered a classroom environment conducive to learning and promoting excellent student/ teacher interaction.

Washington Elementary School - Anytown, MS   *1/95- 6/98*
Classroom Volunteer
- Assisted with reading and classroom activities for children in the first and second grades.
- Helped students with their lessons and encouraged creativity, high-order thinking, and growth potential by means of tutoring/mentoring.
- Promoted a successful learning environment by helping to maintain classroom order and discipline.
- Developed strong practical teaching skills by observing experienced teachers in a classroom setting.

Awards & Affiliations:
- Member, National Association for Future Teachers (NAFT)
- 2002 Youth Leader of the Year, New Light Leadership Coalition (NLLC)

Computer Skills: Proficient in use of Windows, WordPerfect, Word, FrameMaker, Lotus 123, and other spreadsheet software programs

References: Available upon request.

Figure 4.3: Sample **Resume**

Resume Formatting
- Body text should be in standard font (e.g. Times New Roman 12 point).
- Use italics only to highlight a particular aspect of an accomplishment
- Use bold **OR** underline to emphasize a header; do not use them together.
- Standard office paper is acceptable for most positions.
- Do not use colored paper or colored ink for your resume.

Resume Writing Tips

A resume should be:
- Geared toward the industry or company targeted.
- One page in length (preference) – 2 pages (acceptable).
- Free of typos and spelling mistakes
- Brief and clear in content.

Do not:
- Use the word I.
- Refer to yourself by name.
- Include irrelevant information
- Use the phrase "same as above."
- Show frequent changes in employment.

Focus on:
- Qualifying skills.
- Education, training or related experience.
- List of certifications, licenses or languages spoken.
- Employment highlights.
- Pattern of growth or increased responsibilities.
- List of accomplishments, awards, nominations or honors

Figure 4.4: Resume Writing Tips

JOB INTERVIEWS

The job interview is one of the most important steps in getting the job you want. Employers take this opportunity to get to meet the *real* you, not just words printed on a page. During the interview, just relax and be yourself. Don't try to recite what appears on your resume or application. Here are some tips on how to prepare for a successful interview:

1) Research the company by visiting the corporate website or interviewing a current employee. The more you know about your future employer the better.

2) Make sure you know what the position you are applying for entails. Highlight your strengths and talents. Think about what you can offer the company.

3) Dress conservatively. While the company may have a business-casual policy, it is not a good idea to show up at an interview in khakis and a polo shirt. Be as professional as possible--dress down after you get the job.

After you've done all of your research and prepared properly, the day of the interview will arrive.

DO
- Arrive 10 minutes early
- Bring a copy of your resume with you
- Maintain eye contact during the interview and smile

- Firmly shake the interviewer's hand
- Be polite at all times
- Appear confident but not arrogant
- Ask questions about the position
- Talk about yourself and your accomplishments
- Be prepared for tough questions
- End the interview by reiterating your interest in the job
- Send a thank you note to the interviewer

DON'T
- Don't try to interview the interviewer
- Don't try too hard (i.e. bringing diplomas, awards, and bulky portfolios)
- Don't be vague, answer every question with as much detail as possible
- Don't ask at the first opportunity about salaries and benefits
- Don't bring food or drink
- If you had a bad experience at your last job, don't convey that in your interview

Interview Q & A
The first question is straightforward enough and is intended to put the interviewee at ease. A brief description of experiences relevant to the job applied for is enough. The interviewer is not really asking for your life story.

Common Interview Questions & How to Answer

Tell me about yourself.
How to Answer - If this is asked at the beginning of the interview give a quick run down of your qualifications and experience to date, then ask whether the interviewer(s) would like you to expand. If the question is asked towards the end of the interview and you have already talked a lot about yourself, then this is the opportunity for you to elaborate on any positive points and put across any messages you have not had the chance to give so far.

Why did you apply for this position?
How to Answer - Explain why you are interested in the company. If you have had a long-term interest in them, say so. If location is significant, you could mention this after talking about your interest in the firm. Try not to focus on what you will get from the company, but the qualities you will bring to them. You could mention that you see the position as offering challenge, a chance to learn new things and to enhance and develop skills and abilities necessary for the position.

What are your strengths and weaknesses?
How to Answer - Once again the employer is seeking to ascertain how mature you are and your awareness of yourself as a person. If you have a job description, you may find it useful to focus on where you see your strengths and weaknesses in relation to the tasks listed. Remember weaknesses can be turned into strengths. Talk about the strategies you use for dealing with that weakness or its positive side e.g. taking time to make decisions may slow you down, but on the other hand you are not impulsive. Listing too many weaknesses will type you as very negative. You may have to admit that you do not have a particular type of experience called for however you may be able

---

to give evidence of your ability to determine the skills required. Don't bring up too many weaknesses - one or two will suffice!

How long do you expect to stay with us?

How to Answer - Do not commit yourself to a specific time unless you are quite clear on this. Indicate you anticipate staying in the position for as long as it takes to learn the job and to gain experience in it, and that you then hope to move on within the company. After making a comment yourself, you can always turn this question back to the employer and ask how long they would expect you to stay with them.

What do you see yourself doing in five years from now?

How to Answer - Your answer will give evidence of whether or not you are the sort of person who plans ahead. Remember that fewer and fewer employers expect all their employees to make a life-long career in their organization. You may want to express a desire to progress as rapidly as ability and opportunities allow within the organization, or what you would like to do on a broader scale.

Why should we hire you?

How to Answer - Answer in terms of the skills and personal qualities you have relevant to the job. You may refer to your academic qualifications, relevant sections of university courses, experience in the workplace, leisure activities or personal qualities.

How do you get along with other people?

How to Answer - This question is asked to find out more about your social and interpersonal skills. Quote examples of past participation in teams, committees or community organizations. Avoid discussing reasons why you do not get on with certain people. This is a good opportunity to give evidence of any situations that you may have had to use skills of negotiation, motivation or conflict resolution.

CHAPTER 4 REVIEW QUESTIONS

1. Name three important factors to consider when choosing a career.

    *   _____

    *   _____

    *   _____

2. Choosing a College.

    a. What are some good reasons for choosing a college? _____

    _____

    _____

    b. What are some bad reasons for choosing a college? _____

    _____

    _____

3. Name three things you should do to prepare for a job interview.

    *   _____

    *   _____

    *   _____

4. What study habits would you recommend to an auditory learner? _____

    _____

    _____

    _____

5. How would you answer the interview question: *"Why should we hire you?"* ___

    _____

    _____

    _____

    _____

CHAPTER 4 ACTIVITIES

1. Quiz: Assessing Your Learning Style

If you agree with the statement, place a check in the box. If you do not agree with the statement, leave the box empty.

Part A

❑ People say you have terrible handwriting.

❑ You don't like silent filmstrips or charades.

❑ You can spell out loud better than when you have to write it down.

❑ You would rather listen to a tape than watch a film

❑ You like riddles better than cartoons.

❑ Composing music is more exciting than painting a picture

❑ You sometimes leave out words when writing, or sometimes you get words or letters backwards.

❑ You remember things that you talked about in class much better than things that you have read.

❑ You do not like copying notes from the chalkboard or a transparency.

❑ You like games with action or noises better than chess or other board games.

❑ You understand better when you read aloud rather than to yourself.

❑ Sometimes you make math mistakes because you don't notice a (+/-) sign or because you read the numbers/directions wrong.

❑ You hate to read from the computer, especially when the backgrounds are busy.

❑ It is difficult for you to keep neat notes.

❑ It seems like you are the last one to notice something new – i.e. a new poster was placed on the wall in a hallway

❑ You hate geography and map activities.

❑ You use your finger as a pointer when you read.

❑ You often hum or sing to yourself when you are working.

❑ Sometimes your eyes just bother you, but your eye test was normal, or, you have glasses that your eye doctor says are right for you.

❑ Test questions that require matching are hard to sort out.

❑ Sometimes when you read you mix up words that look similar (this/thin or them/the).

Part B

❑ It seems like you always have to ask someone to repeat what he/she just said

❑ Sometimes you find yourself staring out the window when you were really trying to pay attention to something.

❑ Often you know what you want to say, but you just can't think of the words. Sometimes you may even be accused of talking with your hands or calling something a "watchamacallit."

❑ You have been in speech therapy some time previously (or currently).

Copyright © 2001 New Light Leadership Coalition, Inc.   *All Rights Reserved*

❑ You may have trouble understanding a person who is talking to you when you are unable to watch the person's face while he or she is speaking.

❑ You would rather receive directions in a demonstration format than in spoken form.

❑ When you watch TV or listen to the radio, someone is always asking you to turn it down.

❑ Your family/friends say that you say "Huh?" or "What?" too much.

❑ You would rather demonstrate how to do something than explain it.

❑ Spoken words that sound similar (or/are, there/their, Mary/marry) are hard for you to tell apart.

❑ You have pictures or artwork on your notebooks and folders

❑ You have trouble remembering things unless you write them down.

❑ You like board games such as checkers better than listening games.

❑ Sometimes you make mistakes when speaking (like saying, "He got expended from school.").

❑ You like artwork better than music.

❑ You have to go over most of the alphabet in order to remember whether T comes before Q.

❑ You like it better when someone shows you what to do rather than just telling you.

❑ You usually answer questions with yes or no rather than with complete sentences.

❑ You can do many things that are hard to explain with words (like fixing machines or doing other complicated projects).

❑ Often you forget to give verbally received messages (such as telephone messages) to people unless you write them down.

❑ You are always drawing little pictures on the edges of your papers, or doodling on scratch paper.

Scoring:

Give yourself one point for each box that you checked. Add up your score for parts A&B.

Part A Score_____   Part B Score_____

Compare your scores for each section:
- If your part A score is very much higher than your part B score, then you could be considered an **auditory learner**.
- If your part B score is much higher, it indicates that you are most likely a **visual learner**.
- If both your part B and part A scores are high, your best learning mode would probably be touching and doing **(kinesthetic learner)**.

[This instrument is adapted from Puzzled About Educating Special Needs Students by the Wisconsin Centre on Education and Work (1980)]

---

2. **Scholarship Search**

⌨ *WWW Activity:* Fill out a personal profile at Fastweb.com - http://www.fastweb.com Try to find at least 5 scholarships you qualify for and print out the information for each one. Keep track of when you will apply for each scholarship in the boxes below.

- OR -

Go to your local library and ask the librarian for their newest copies of scholarship directories. Most of these books are reference so you will not be able to check them out. Find at least 7 scholarships you qualify for and take down the following information for each:

Example

Name of Scholarship: *Youth Leader of the Year Award*

Organization/School: *New Light Leadership Coalition*

Application Deadline: *September 30, 2003* Date Sent: *August 15, 2003*

Short Description: *Write a one-page essay on the principles of leadership development.* _____ Award Amount: *Varies*

Name of Scholarship: _____

Organization/School: _____

Application Deadline: _____ Date Sent: _____

Short Description: _____ Award $: _____

Name of Scholarship: _____

Organization/School: _____

Application Deadline: _____ Date Sent: _____

Short Description: _____ Award $: _____

Name of Scholarship: _____

Organization/School: _____

Application Deadline: _____ Date Sent: _____

Short Description: _____ Award $: _____

Name of Scholarship: _____

Organization/School: _____

Application Deadline: _____ Date Sent: _____

Short Description: _____ Award $: _____

Name of Scholarship: _____

Organization/School: _____

Application Deadline: _____ Date Sent: _____

Short Description: _____ Award $: _____

Name of Scholarship: _____

Organization/School: _____

Application Deadline: _____ Date Sent: _____

Short Description: _____ Award $: _____

---

3. **Writing Your Resume**
Refer to the section on resume writing in this workbook. To build your resume, think about your past work experience. If you do not have any work experience, think about organizations you have been involved in and any volunteer work you have done. Use a wordprocessor like Microsoft Word or Word Perfect to write your resume.

⌨ *WWW Activity:* Go to **www.jobdirect.com** and build an online resume.

⌨ *WWW Activity:* Go to **www.collegegrad.com/resumes** for suggestions for improving your resume.

4. **Interview a Company**
Contact the human resources department of a company you would like to work for. Ask if you can schedule an informational interview to find out more information about what the company has to offer. Try to have a specific position or department in mind so you can be directed to talk to the appropriate person. This is a great way to learn about a company without directly asking for a job. It is also a good idea for students who want to work in a particular industry or field that want a real life view of how it operates. Be sure to ask questions about the company environment, opportunities for advancement, and the duties of certain positions.

5. **Take a College Tour**
Visit one of your top 3 college choices. Often colleges have pre-college programs for high school students or specific weekends of activities for students interested in attending their institution. Have a list of questions ready to ask your tour guide or the admissions office representative present during your tour. This will give you a better idea about the school you plan to attend. A good way to get a more realistic perspective not found in the brochure is to interview a student that attends the college. Ask them about their expectations of the school versus what happened once they became students. Students are not trying to get you to enroll in the school so they will be more open and honest with you.

CHAPTER 4 PROJECTS

Project 1: **Educational Choices**

High School Students:
1. Write down the qualities that are important for the college you will go to. Below are some things you may want to consider:

Location	**Available Majors**	**Accredited Programs**
Size	**Urban, Rural, Suburban**	**Diversity**
Average SAT's	**Graduation/Drop-out Rate**	**Reputation**

2. Visit www.collegeboard.org or go to your local library and research the colleges you are considering. Determine if the colleges fit into the criteria you have defined. List your schools and as you do your research, place a (+) next to each school when it has a criteria you like and a (-) when there is something you dislike about the school.

3. Add up all of your (+) and (-) for each school. Rank the choices in order from the school with the most important qualities to the one with none or little of the qualities you think are important for a school.
        a. What is your top choice?
        b. What is your last choice?
        c. What did you learn by going through using this process?

College/Post-secondary Students:
Project A
1. Write down the qualities that are important in the company you want to work for.
2. Write down three companies that you have considered working for.
3. Go to the each company's website place a check next to each.

Project B
1. Write down the things that are important to you in choosing the career or field you are interested in pursuing. Here are some things you might want to consider:

Environment	**Advancement Opportunities**
Salary	**Current State of the Field**
Diversity in Field	**Working with People**

2. Write down the three top careers you have considered.
3. Research the careers you have selected. The Bureau of Labor Statistics website (http://stats.bls.gov) is a good place to look. You can also go to your local library and find the Occupational Outlook Handbook published by the Bureau of Labor Statistics. Determine if each career has the qualities that you consider favorable. As you do your research, place a (+) next to each career when it has a criteria you like and a (-) when there is something you dislike about it.
4. Add up all of your (+) and (-) and rank the choices in order from the school with the most important qualities to the one with none or little of the qualities you think are important for a career.
    a. What is your top choice?
    b. What is your last choice?
5. What did you learn by going through using this process?
6. Did you change your top career choice? Why or why not?

Project 2: **Personal Leadership Plan: Part III**
What are your goals for educational development? After reading this chapter, pick something you would like to work on as it relates to your educational development. Refer back to the sample on page 31 to help with this project.

Personal Leadership Plan: Part III

Educational Development Goal(s): _____

_____

_____

_____

What has stopped me from accomplishing this goal?

_____

_____

Objectives - *What do I have to do in order to meet my overall goal?*

• _____

• _____

• _____

Action Items - *What steps will I take to fulfill my objectives?*

• _____

• _____

• _____

Outcomes - *What happened as a result of your action plan?*

• _____

• _____

• _____

Evaluation - *Did I meet my goal? How can I improve my approach in the future?*

_____

SUGGESTED READING FOR CHAPTER 4

1. <u>Black College Student Survival Guide</u> by Jawanza Kunjufu

2. <u>The Mis-education of the Negro</u> by Carter G. Woodson

3. <u>Best Buys in College Education</u> by Lucia Solorzano

4. <u>Best Answers to the 201 Most Frequently Asked Interview Questions</u> by Matthew J. Deluca

5. <u>Test Your Own Job Aptitude : Exploring Your Career Potential</u> by James Barrett, Geoff Williams

CHAPTER 5: ECONOMIC DEVELOPMENT

TOPICS IN ECONOMIC DEVELOPMENT

- Budgeting Your Money
- Establishing Credit
- Saving & Investing
- Entrepreneurship

CHAPTER 5: ECONOMIC DEVELOPMENT

Key Terms for Economic Development

1. **401(K)** A retirement investment plan that allows an employee to put a percentage of earned wages into a tax-deferred investment account selected by the employer

2. **BOND** a certificate of debt issued by a government or corporation guaranteeing payment of the original investment plus interest by a specified future date.

3. **BUDGET** an estimate, often itemized, of expected income and expense for a given period in the future

4. **BUSINESS** the purchase and sale of goods and services in an attempt to make a profit

5. **BUSINESS PLAN** a document prepared by a company's management, detailing the past, present, and future of the company, usually designed to attract capital investment

6. **CAPITAL** material wealth used or available for use in the production of more wealth

7. **CREDIT RATING** a classification of credit risk based on investigation of a customer's or potential customer's financial resources, prior payment pattern, and personal history or degree of personal responsibility for debts incurred.

8. **CREDITOR** a person or firm to whom money is due

9. **CURRENCY** something that is used as a medium of exchange; money

10. **DEBT** something that is owed or that one is bound to pay to or perform for another

11. **ECONOMIC** pertaining to the production, distribution, and use of income, wealth, and commodities.

12. **EXPENSE** cost or charge

13. **EMPOWER** to enable or permit

14. **ENTREPRENEUR** a person who organizes and manages any enterprise, esp. a business, usually with considerable initiative and risk

15. **INCOME** the monetary payment received for goods or services, or from other sources, as rents or investments

16. **INTEREST** An excess or bonus beyond what is expected or due, usually a percentage

17. **INVESTMENT** property or another possession acquired for future financial return or benefit

---

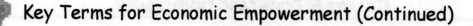

Key Terms for Economic Empowerment (Continued)

18. IRA (INDIVIDUAL RETIREMENT ACCOUNT) a self-funded retirement plan that allows you to contribute a limited yearly sum toward your retirement; taxes on the interest earned in the account are deferred

19. LOAN something borrowed for *temporary* use

20. MANAGE to handle, direct, govern, or control in action or use

21. PROFIT 1. an advantageous gain or return; benefit. 2. the return received on a business undertaking after all operating expenses have been met.

22. PORTFOLIO a group of investments.

23. STOCK The capital or fund that a corporation raises through the sale of shares entitling the stockholder to dividends and to other rights of ownership, such as voting rights

24. WORTH 1. having value 2. wealth; riches; property or possessions: *net worth.*

BUDGETING YOUR MONEY

THE IMPORTANCE OF BUDGETING

Budgeting is the process of rationing the money you earn while keeping future expenditures in mind. Most people think a **budget** is a trap, restricting how you spend your money. The reason budgeting has a negative connotation to it is because you expect that you will feel limited in what you can do with your money. The truth is you can be as flexible or rigid with your own budget as you would like. After all, it is your money and you ultimately will decide what to do with it. A budget is a guide for some of your financial goals. While it does take some time and planning, you must prepare a budget if you plan to be a successful manager of your money.

YOUR PERSONAL BUDGET

There are many approaches to budgeting. You may decide to budget your money daily, weekly, or even monthly. Budgets can range from one year to up to five years or more. Your short-term **investments** and expenditures will appear in a one-year budget while more major investments, such as deciding to buy a house or a car, may be included in a long-term five-year plan. Here are some things to remember when planning a budget:

1. A Budget is a Plan
It is important to remember a budget is a plan. You must set clear, concise goals in order for your budget to be effective.

2. Be Realistic
Know your limitations and areas of potential improvement. If you set outlandish goals for your budget or make it too detailed to follow, it will probably fail. Increase your chances of success by allowing for flexibility in your budget. For example, instead of setting the goal to spend $25.50 per week on food, you may want to set a range between $20 to $30 for food **expenses**. This is much more realistic than trying to meet an exact amount every week.

3. Condense Your Expenses
Look for ways to save money. If you eat out everyday for lunch, try packing a lunch to save on food expenses. If you buy junk food from vending machines on a regular basis, think of the money you would save if you purchased a large bag of snacks from the store at the same price a small bag costs in the vending machine. You may also decide to sacrifice shopping sprees and impulse purchases. Try not to succumb to advertisements that say 50% - 75% off. Sales can save you money, but some stores raise their prices a week prior to a big sale so in the end you really are not saving money, but just getting the retail price in the first place. Discipline yourself to be mindful about the way you spend your money.

4. Pay Yourself First
Get into the habit of paying yourself first. Set aside some money for savings each time you receive income from a paycheck or allowance. Develop a system of savings

Copyright © 2001 New Light Leadership Coalition, Inc.   All Rights Reserved that works for you. It is recommended that you choose a certain amount or percentage, such as $25 per month or 20% of every pay period. Also consider the money you spend on charity and donations. Add this money to your budget also so you will always be prepared to give without sacrificing other bills.

5. **Stick to Your Plan**

As with any plan, budgeting must be followed through. Setting budget goals will only be successful to the degree that you see each goal through. If you miss one month of savings or spend too much money one week, get right back on track with your budget. Do not allow splurges or unexpected expenses to take you away from your overall budget goals. Re-evaluate your budget as time goes by and as your incomes and expenses change.

In the end, your net **worth** or **value** is determined by the amount of **capital** minus the amount of **debt** you have accumulated in your lifetime. Getting an early start to good money management practices will ensure a healthy financial future.

BUDGETING FOR A PROJECT OR ORGANIZATION

When preparing a budget for a project or organization you have many things to consider. The main question is what is your source of funding and what will it be used for?

A budget must always be prepared in advance and all expenses must be justified. A good place to start is with the previous year's budget. Consider what has changed from the previous year. Are there more expenses because of new programs and initiatives? Is there a greater source of income due to increased membership? If you are starting a new organization or project and have to build your budget from scratch, try to find out what similar organizations' or projects' expenses are. The best way is to do your own independent research into how much things will actually cost and assessing what is essential to get your project or organization off the ground.

In larger organizations, each committee will submit a budget to the Treasurer or Executive Board for the upcoming year's expenses. When chairing a committee or project, keep receipts for everything and make sure you have a valid reason for requesting funds. The Board will usually decide what funds you receive so keep it simple and look for ways to save money for your organization.

Community-based organizations depend on membership dues, grants, and other in-kind donations for support. Most student organizations receive a budget from the Student Government but oftentimes that is not enough to fund an entire year of projects. Even if SGA funding covers all of your organization's expenses, the Student Government may require you to raise a percentage of those funds on your own. Fundraising efforts are an important part of budget planning for any project or organization. Look for creative ways to raise money and think outside of the box. Hosting events that are relatively inexpensive but have the potential to bring revenue from outside sources can be a good way to generate funds. Try not to depend solely on the members for financial support, especially if they already have an obligation to pay dues. Finding ways to form partnerships with other organizations and companies can help offset expenses and give your organization greater exposure. Make sure partnerships are mutually beneficial to both parties involved.

CREDIT

WHAT IS YOUR CREDIT SCORE?

Credit scoring is a point system used to determine whether or not you should be extended credit, or the luxury of receiving a product now and paying for it later. Many companies use your credit score or rating to determine your ability to repay them. Your past payment history, current salary, and job history can play a role in your credit rating.

To find our your credit score, check with one of the 3 major companies:

Equifax: 1-800-685-1111 *www. equifax.com*
Experian (formerly TRW): 1-800-682-7654
Trans-Union: 1-800-916-8800

You can also find your credit rating online for free at certain websites. Most young people are financially handicapped because they fail to establish credit. You will find that having no credit is almost as bad as having bad credit. Look for ways to build your credit without going deep into debt that you cannot handle. If you do not have any bills in your name, you essentially have no credit. A good first step might be to get a phone line turned on in your name and make your payments on time. The next section will discuss some ways you can establish credit.

ESTABLISHING CREDIT

1. **Pay your bills on time.**
    This is the most important factor in determining your credit score. An occasional late payment is OK, however, having too many late payments or payments over 60 days-late can have a negative effect on your credit score and cause you to lose points.

2. **Be patient.**
    Building a solid credit history takes time. To build up a good credit rating will take years of good credit practices.

3. **Don't get into debt.**
    A large amount of debt can prevent you from opening new accounts.

4. **Avoid inquiries.**
    Every time you apply for a credit card or a loan, an inquiry will appear on your credit report. Keep the number of inquiries on your credit file to a minimum. Too many inquiries will increase your credit risk.

5. **Check your credit report for errors.**
    Sometimes companies fail to report changes in your account status to the credit bureau. Make sure your credit history is accurate. If you have a delinquent account that is finally paid off, request a letter from the company stating that your account is

again in good standing. This letter will help you settle any dispute about an old account balance appearing on your credit report.

You can also build credit by getting a credit card. Major credit cards are better than store cards and usually carry lower interest rates. Once you turn eighteen, companies will bombard you with credit card offers. Most college students go into debt with student loans and credit cards and find it hard to dig themselves out of that hole after graduation. Remember, whatever you spend you have to pay for. Get a card with a low credit limit, somewhere around $500, and use that to establish some credit history. Keep in mind that if you pay all bills back within 30 days, most companies will not charge you any interest at all. Be responsible with your first credit card and establish a good relationship with the credit card company. After you make your payments on time for at least one year, call the credit card company and ask them to reduce your interest rate. Most of the time, they will say yes.

Possible reasons for a lower credit rating

Credit ratings are very complex, but some of the most common factors that can affect your score in a negative way are:

- *Amount owed on accounts is too high.*
- *Delinquency on accounts.*
- *Too few bank revolving accounts.*
- *Too many bank or national revolving accounts.*
- *Too many accounts with balances.*
- *Consumer finance accounts.*
- *Account payment history too new to rate.*
- *Too many recent inquiries in the last 12 months.*
- *Too many accounts opened in the last 12 months.*
- *Proportion of balances to credit limits is too high on revolving accounts.*
- *Amount owed on revolving accounts is too high.*
- *Length of revolving credit history is too short.*
- *Time since delinquency is too recent or unknown.*
- *Length of credit history is too short.*
- *Lack of recent bank revolving information.*
- *Lack of recent revolving account information.*
- *No recent non-mortgage balance information.*

- *Number of accounts with delinquency.*
- *Too few accounts currently paid as agreed.*
- *Time since derogatory public record or collection.*
- *Amount past due on accounts.*
- *Serious delinquency, derogatory public record, or collection.*
- *Too many bank or national revolving accounts with balances.*
- *No recent revolving balances.*
- *Proportion of loan balances to loan amounts is too high.*
- *Lack of recent installment loan information.*
- *Date of last inquiry too recent.*
- *Time since most recent account opening too short.*
- *Number of revolving accounts.*
- *Number of bank revolving or other revolving accounts.*
- *Number of established accounts.*
- *No recent bankcard balances.*
- *Too few accounts with recent payment information*

Saving & Investing

Many of us believe that being a millionaire is a goal that cannot be achieved by the "average" person. In fact, now is the best time to start thinking about **saving** your money. The more time you have the more your money will grow in the long run and as a young person, you have to take charge of your finances now.

The key to making money is letting your money work _for_ you. When you earn money, you can either a) spend it or b) save it. It's that simple. The more you save the more you will have in the long run.

There are many options available to help you earn **interest** in your money. You will find that you will earn more interest on investments that are more risky. You can use the rule of 70 to determine how long it will take your money to double at a given interest rate. No matter what the initial dollar amount invested, the rule of 70 will let you know how long it will take that amount to grow to twice the initial deposit.

Rule of 70: Divide any interest rate by 70 to determine the number of years it will take your money to double.

Example: You invest some money into a savings account that gives you an interest rate of 1.5%.

$$70 \div 1.5 = 46.66667$$

Using the rule of 70, we learn that it will take almost 47 years for your money to double at a 1.5-% interest rate.

Investment Options

Several options are available to help you save your money. Below is a listing and description of different types of accounts you can select when deciding to become an investor.

Savings & Money Market Accounts
Most banks offer savings accounts to individuals that require low minimum balances. Usually, these are a very low risk investment and pay low interest rates. Money market accounts offer higher interest rates than regular savings accounts but require higher minimum balances.

Certificates of Deposit (CDs)
CDs are purchased for specific amounts of money at a fixed rate of interest for a specific amount of time. CDs may be purchased for as little as $500 but generally are priced at $1,000, $5,000, or $10,000. You may buy a CD for as little time as a few days, or for as long as several years. The longer time usually carries a higher interest rate. If you cash in the CD before the specified time, you will have to pay penalties.

Mutual Funds

A **mutual fund** is an investment company that continually offers new shares and buys existing shares back at the request of the shareholder and uses its capital to invest in diversified securities of other companies. A financial service company may offer a number of funds with different objectives.

Stocks

A **stock** is the capital or fund that a corporation raises through the sale of shares entitling the stockholder to dividends and to other rights of ownership, such as voting rights. When you own shares of stock you become part owner of a company. If the company does well, the value of your stock should go up over time. If the company does not do well, the value of your investment will decrease. Most companies distribute a portion of their profits to shareholders as dividends. There are different types of stock and it is best to use a financial planner to help you make the decision on which stocks to buy. Since there is a higher risk in stock investments, the interest rates earned on stocks are usually higher also.

Bonds

A **bond** is a certificate of debt issued by a government or corporation guaranteeing payment of the original investment plus interest by a specified future date. When you own a bond you have loaned money to a company or a governmental unit. In return, the borrower promises to repay the amount borrowed plus interest. Publicly owned companies issue corporate bonds, while state or local governments issue municipal bonds.

CHOOSING A FINANCIAL INSTITUTION

Financial institutions are businesses that offer services such as checking and savings accounts, car loans, home mortgages, credit cards, and retirement and investment services. There are several types of financial institutions: banks, savings and loan associations and credit unions. Many of these institutions offer the same services.

Banks and savings and loan associations (S&Ls) are businesses that operate under federal and state laws. They are closely regulated so your money is safe. They offer loans, credit cards, safe deposit boxes, investment services, and checking and savings accounts that are insured by the federal government.

Credit unions are not-for-profit, member-owned cooperatives

BANKS VS. CREDIT UNIONS		
	Advantages	**Disadvantages**
Banks and Savings & Loans	• ATM Access • Many Branch Locations	• High Fees • Less personalized service
Credit Union	• Low or virtually no fees • High interest paid • Low financing interest rates	• Low ATM Access • Few Branch Locations

that operate under federal or state laws. They serve members who have something in common, such as working for the same employer, belonging to the same group or living in the same community. They are closely regulated so your money is safe. Most credit unions offer loans, credit cards, and checking (share draft) and savings (share) accounts that are insured by the federal government.

Questions to Consider When Choosing a Financial Institution

- ◆ *Does it offer services I need?*
  - ◆ *What kind of ID is required to open an account?*
    - ◆ *What fees will I be charged on a monthly basis?*
      - ◆ *Is it close to home?*
        - ◆ *Is it open when I need it to be?*
          - ◆ *Does it have ATMs in convenient locations?*
            - ◆ *Can I join a credit union?*
              - ◆ *Do the employees speak my language?*

Copyright © 2001 New Light Leadership Coalition, Inc.   *All Rights Reserved*   Page 107

ENTREPRENEURSHIP

This section will give you some insight into how a business is started. If you are seriously interested in starting your own business, consult the *Suggested Reading for Economic Development* section for more in-depth sources of information.

ENTREPRENEURS ARE LEADERS

Entrepreneur is a French word that literally means *one who takes risks*. An entrepreneur is a person that starts their own business. This person must also play a significant role in the ownership and operations of that business. The dictionary definition of entrepreneur is *a person who organizes and manages any enterprise, especially a business, usually with considerable initiative and risk.*

Entrepreneurs are leaders. It requires innovation and risk-taking to start a business venture that may or may not be successful. The statistics say that most business start-ups fail and even those that are profitable may not make any money until the third year of operation. It requires leadership, optimism, and vision to be able to see an idea through until it is complete. Starting a business takes time and effort and oftentimes, if you are the one with the idea you will be the one to work the hardest on it.

TYPES OF BUSINESSES

When most people think of business they think of corporations. Corporations are popular because they are perceived to be the largest businesses and most recognizable, however, corporation doesn't mean "big." In fact, the majority of businesses in this country are small businesses and many small businesses do have corporate status. You may not think of the gas station or candy store on the corner as big businesses, but most of them are incorporated.

A Corporation is a business that is its own legal entity. That means it can write checks, buy and sell property and products, and own things just as a person can. Corporations are fairly easy to start but have many regulations. It only requires paying a filing fee to your state and drafting your articles of incorporation. The articles of incorporation or charter is a set of laws that govern how your business will function and are composed much like bylaws or the constitution of a student organization. A corporation's income is taxed just as a person's income. There are also different types of corporations and each has their own set of requirements. Nonprofit corporations such as churches, universities, foundations, and community organizations do not have to pay federal taxes because they are providing a service for the good of the community. Although nonprofits are not in existence to make money, it is still run like a business. It must raise money to continue serving its constituents.

Many people choose to incorporate because of the liability involved with starting a business. If a product or service fails, it is better for the business owner if the company is sued and not the business owner. While the company may lose all of its assets and go out of business as a result of a lawsuit or other complaint, the individual's assets, such as a car, house, and personal savings are protected. Another advantage of a corporation is the ability to sell shares of stock to raise money for business operations.

Another type of business is a partnership. The most common examples of partnerships are doctor's offices, law firms, and accountants. A partnership allows you to share liability or responsibility for the business' assets with one or more people. To form a partnership you need a written partnership agreement signed by all partners. This usually indicates who operates the business and the percentages of ownership and profit sharing.

The most simple business form is the sole proprietorship. A sole proprietorship is a business with one owner. The owner of a sole proprietorship is usually liable for anything that happens with the business but has the luxury of keeping all of the profits. There are, however, limited resources in this form of business. Usually the business owner does all of the work with little or no help. Good examples of sole proprietorships are consulting services such as financial planners, management consultants, and tax preparation services.

STEPS TO STARTING A BUSINESS

After you choose which type of business is best for your business idea, there are some steps you have to take to begin operating a business legally.

1. Write a Business Plan
Most new businesses fail. There are many factors contributing to their failure, but one is lack of planning. A business plan is a document detailing the past, present, and future of the company and is usually designed to attract potential investors. Depending on the scope of your new venture, you will need to write a **business plan** and may want to consult your local Small Business Administration (SBA) office and your city's Chamber of Commerce. These groups provide help and resources to new businesses and sometimes offer financial and legal advice for free through mentorships and workshops. To find your local SBA office, look in your phone book or go to http://www.sba.gov. A business plan determines how your business is run and usually includes an executive summary (mission statement and vision for the company), explanation of the competitive advantage, management structure and qualifications, financial plan for up to five years, short- and long-term goals, and a clear explanation of your business model. A business model outlines how you plan to make money. Who will pay for your product or service? How much will they pay? How many sales will you make in a given period? What expenses will you incur to provide your product or service? Many businesses are not profitable in the first three years as they build customer loyalty and increase sales. Investors will want to know how you plan to become and remain profitable and competitive in the market, so a business plan is essential for any new venture.

2. Check with your state
Each state has its own requirements for starting a business. You can find information for your state by going to: http://www.taxadmin.org/fta/forms.ssi
In Maryland, the State Department of Assessments and Taxation handles all business services. A checklist for starting a business in Maryland is available on their website at: **http://www.dat.state.md.us/sdatweb/checklist.html** or contact them at: State Department of Assessments and Taxation, Corporate Charter Division, 301 West Preston Street, Rm. 809, Baltimore, MD 21201, Telephone: (410) 767-1340.

3. Select a Business Name

Choose a name for your business. Once you decide what you will call your new enterprise, check with your state office again to do a trade name or corporate name search. This is to make sure no one else is currently using that name to avoid any confusion or possible legal action. After choosing a unique business name register it with your state. This will give you the rights to use that name in your state and prevent others from starting a business with your name.

4. Obtain a Federal Tax ID Number

In order to complete the registration process for your business with the state, you must first register your business at the federal level and obtain a Federal Employer Identification Number (FEIN). Even if you do not have employees you must register your business with the federal government. You can obtain the FEIN application (Form SS-4) at your local IRS office, by calling 1-800-829-3676, or going online: http://www.irs.ustreas.gov/forms_pubs/index.html

5. Research Local, State, and Federal Tax Laws

Businesses have to pay taxes for buying and selling products and services. Usually, the IRS and your state will send you the proper forms and notify you of the tax requirements for your business. If your business is fairly small, you may be able to read the publications and forms for yourself and file the taxes for your business; however, it is best to consult a professional accountant to handle your taxes for you. Many states have sales taxes. In Maryland, you have to charge your customer a 5% sales tax and turn that money over to the state government. Usually, the federal tax rate for businesses is 25% of the profits per year. If the business has a net loss at the end of the year, meaning the total revenues for the year were less than the total expenses, it does not have a heavy tax burden.

Small Business Resource (Federal): http://www.irs.gov/smallbiz/index.htm
Small Business Resource (Maryland State): http://business.marylandtaxes.com

6. Run Your Business

With any plan, the execution is the most important part and can be the most difficult. It is a challenge to start a business from scratch. Make sure you are in business not just for the money, but because it is something you genuinely enjoy. The more passionate you are about your business the more that will translate to others and they will enjoy doing business with you. Finding the time to work on your business is also another challenge. If you work at a regular job and and/or attend school, your time is already scarce. Running a business requires a commitment on your part. If you have business partners you can divide responsibilities between all of you and it could make your load lighter. You may want to start only working on your business part-time to see how things go. Or, you may want to conduct a survey to see if there is interest in your idea. After you have tested the market you may decide not to invest time in money into an idea that is not working or you may experience success and take the final step to running your business on a full-time basis. Whatever you decide, follow through with your business plan and stay focused.

Copyright © 2001 New Light Leadership Coalition, Inc. *All Rights Reserved*

CHAPTER 5 REVIEW QUESTIONS

1. Why is budgeting important? _____

_____

_____

2. What are the benefits of using a credit union as opposed to a bank?

_____

_____

_____

3. If you wanted to start an internship search service, what type of business (corporation, sole proprietorship, or partnership) would you use and why?

_____

_____

_____

4. Is getting a credit card a good way to establish credit? Why or why not?

_____

_____

_____

5. What should you consider when budgeting for an organization or special project?

_____

_____

_____

_____

CHAPTER 5 ACTIVITIES

1. 💻 *WWW Activity:* Go to **www.freecreditanalyzer.com** and find out your credit rating.

What is your credit rating? _____

What will you do to improve or establish your credit?

_____

_____

_____

_____

2. If you wanted to start a business today, what would it be? Describe a business venture you would like to start.

Name of Business_____

Type of Business_____

Brief Description (What will your business do?)

_____

_____

_____

_____

Target Market: Who will your customers be? (ex. students 14-18 in Maryland)

_____

Competitive Advantage: Why will they buy from you? _____

_____

_____

Start-up Costs: What do you need to start your business?

_____   _____

_____   _____

_____   _____

Marketing Plan: Where will you sell your product or service? *(local stores, online, sell directly to customers, etc.)* _____

_____

_____

How will you market your product? *(advertising in newspapers & magazine, flyers, etc.)*

_____

_____

_____

Set a price for your product: $_____

Questions: Is the price you set for your product able to cover all of the costs associated with producing and advertising the product?

_____

_____

_____

Are people willing to pay that price for your product? Is the price too low or too high?

_____

_____

_____

How much time are you willing to put into your business each week?

_____

_____

CHAPTER 5 PROJECTS

1. Your Budget
Keep track of expenses and income for a week. Below is a sample budget:

Sample Budget

Date	To/From	Memo	Amount	Balance
6/6/01	McDonalds	Paycheck	$150.00	$150.00
6/6/01	Savings Account	Personal Savings	-$15.00	$135.00
6/8/01	Footlocker	New Shoes	-$90.00	$45.00
6/9/01	Grocery Store	Food	-$20.00	$25.00
6/9/01	NLLC	Membership Dues	-$15.00	$5.00

Use this table to keep track of everything you receive and spend for at least one week.

My Budget for the Week of _____

Date	To/From	Memo	Amount	Balance

Budget Questions:

a) How much money did you spend during the week? $_____

b) How much money did you earn or receive during the week? $_____

c) Look at your expenses. What did you spend the most on this week?

_____

d) After doing this exercise, do you think you manage your money well? Why or why not?

_____

_____

_____

e) What will you change about your spending habits in the future?

_____

_____

_____

f) What will you change about your savings habits in the future?

_____

_____

_____

2. Grow Your Money

Go to your local bank and open a savings account. Pledge to yourself to save a certain amount of money every month and deposit it into your account. When you get your bank statement every month, record how much money you save and how much interest you earn each month.

Goal: **I will save $_____ every month.**

Month	Amount Deposited	Interest Earned	Account Balance
	$	$	$
	$	$	$
	$	$	$
	$	$	$
Total After 4 Months	$	$	$

Questions:

a) Look at how much interest you earned over this short time period. What would happen if you continued to save money at this rate for 10 years?

_____

_____

_____

b) In the future will you invest more or less money into this account? Why?

_____

_____

_____

3. **Start or Join an Investment Club**

Most colleges have investment clubs in the school of business and economics. Find out if there is an investment club that you can join at your school or start your own.

⌨ *WWW Activity:* Go to http://www.studentinvestmentclubs.com for information on how to start your own investment club.

4. **Personal Leadership Plan: Part IV -** Use what you learned about goal setting to form a plan for your economic development.

Personal Leadership Plan: Part IV

Economic Development Goal(s): _____

_____

_____

What has stopped me from accomplishing this goal?

_____

_____

Objectives - *What do I have to do in order to meet my overall goal?*

• _____

• _____

• _____

Copyright © 2001 New Light Leadership Coalition, Inc.   *All Rights Reserved*

Action Items - *What steps will I take to fulfill my short-term goals?*

- _____

- _____

- _____

Outcomes - *What happened as a result of your action plan?*

- _____

- _____

- _____

Evaluation - *Did I meet my goal? How can I improve my approach in the future?*

_____

_____

SUGGESTED READING FOR CHAPTER 5

1. Young Entrepreneur's Guide to Owning & Operating a Business by Steve Mariotti

2. The Richest Man in Babylon by George Clason

3. Rich Dad, Poor Dad by Robert T. Kiyosaki

4. An Introduction to Business for African-American Youth by Abner McWhorter, Debra Adams, and Shelby McPherson

5. Get Real!: A Student's Guide to Money & Other Practical Matters by James Tenuto

6. Think & Grow Rich by Napoleon Hill

CHAPTER 6:
POLITICAL DEVELOPMENT

TOPICS IN POLITICAL DEVELOPMENT

- What is Politics?
- Why Youth Should Get Involved
- Steps to Political Activism

CHAPTER 6: POLITICAL DEVELOPMENT

 ## Key Terms for Political Development

1. **ACCESS** to make contact with or gain access to; be able to reach, approach, enter

2. **DEMOCRACY** a form of government in which the supreme power is vested in the people and exercised directly by them

3. **GOVERNMENT** administration or management of an organization, business, or institution

4. **JUSTICE** 1. the quality of being just; equitable 2. the administering of deserved punishment or reward

5. **LAW** the principles and regulations established in a community by some authority and applicable to its people

6. **POLITICS** 1. the art or science of government 2. competition between competing interest groups or individuals for power and resources

7. **RESOURCE** a source of supply, support, or aid, especially one that can be readily drawn upon when needed.

8. **RIGHT** a just claim or title, whether legal, prescriptive, or moral

9. **SOCIETY** a highly structured system of human organization for large-scale community living that normally furnishes protection, continuity, security, and a national identity for its members

10. **VOTE** a formal expression of opinion or choice, either positive or negative, made by n individual or body of individuals.

WHAT IS POLITICS?

Politics effect all areas of our lives. Our schools, streets, doctors, are all effected by political policies. **Politics** is defined as the science of **government** or the competition between competing interest groups or individuals for power and **resources**. This also includes activities that ensure that power is used in a particular way.

The United States and other countries are said to be run by a **democracy**--a form of government in which the supreme power is vested in the people and exercised directly by them; however, in the United States this is not exactly the case. The function of the US government is ideally a democratic republic. This means that the people elect representatives to speak for them and bring a voice to their concerns.

All political philosophies are just theory that must be carried out and practiced by people that inevitably make mistakes. Any political system is interpreted and run by people and is never exactly the same in theory and in practice. Just reflect on the recent history of America when it was **law** that Black people were only three fifths of a human being. The constitution is a noble document in theory but the practice and sickness of racism was rampant in the people who wrote and interpreted that law. This apparent inconsistency discourages youth and the **society** at large from even dealing with the system.

WHY YOUTH SHOULD GET INVOLVED

Here are some facts about youth involvement in politics in America.
- In 1996, only 49 percent voted in the presidential election.
- Only 32 percent of those 18 to 24 years of age voted.
- In many major American cities, the mayor is elected by less than 10 percent of those eligible to vote.

REGISTER TO VOTE!
Pick up an application at:
- ☑ Your Local Board of Elections Office
- ☑ Local Post Offices
- ☑ Libraries
- ☑ The Motor Vehicle Administration
- ☑ City Government Agencies
- ☑ All Public Assistance Offices
- ☑ Any Office Providing State-Funded Programs

Young people stay away from politics for several reasons. The main two misconceptions are: 1) politics doesn't effect me and; 2) I am too young to vote so I cannot be involved, and even if I can **vote,** my vote doesn't count.

When we think about voting, most of us think about the presidential election. The process by which the president is elected discourages people from voting. Locally, you can elect mayors and governors that will serve your interests. Get involved. Watch the debates and learn about their campaigns.

Youth ages 18 and over can register to vote, but politics is much more than voting. The techniques described in the next section can be applied at the community, university, city, state, and national levels.

STEPS TO POLITICAL ACTIVISM

STEP 1: INVESTIGATE

An ability to **investigate** and research is key for the mastery of political activism. Information is power, and having the right information is key when approaching any issue. The same techniques you employ when writing a research paper are necessary for political activism. Gather information and sort through what is useful and what is not. Consider the source of your information and take into account the biases of the writer. For example, you would not take an article about the slave trade seriously if it were written by the Grand Dragon of the Ku Klux Klan. Know all sides of an issue before reaching a conclusion by consulting different sources.

This is the first and most crucial step in political development because without proper information, you are not empowered to take action. This is a skill that takes time to develop but will only get better with experience, patience, and practice.

- Read, watch, and listen to publications, programs, and radio shows. Most publications are circulated daily, weekly, and monthly. It is also important to watch news programs that focus on local, statewide, national, and international news.

- Develop a broad based newspaper, audio, photographic and video library of public and private issues, and the individuals who where involved in them.

- Create a database of individuals involved in issues that effect the public interest.

- Identify and monitor all print and broadcast media. Locate media outlets that would be willing to allow you to write or host special interest, news and/or community or political issues in a news column or TV or radio forum.

    - Build relationships with people that work for the media (i.e. radio show hosts, journalists, local news personalities, etc.)

    - Communicate via snail mail or email and keep a copy of all correspondence.

    - Learn how to write press releases and public service announcements.

STEP 2: IDENTIFY

Identify key **people**, **institutions**, and **resources**. This will enable you to find out who is in charge of what, what different public institutions do to serve your community, and how resources are allocated.

☞ **People**

Find out the names of every elected or appointed official for the local, state, and even federal governments, along with clergy, community commissioners, ward bosses, heads of organizations, boards, and committees. Find out when their terms are up and if they are planning to run for election, reelection or reappointment. This is important information because officials are more vulnerable and receptive during times of election and appointments.

- What are the main issues are that they support?
- Who do they support?
- What are they against?
- What committees, boards, and commissions to they serve on?

☞ **Institutions**

Form a list of all government offices, neighborhood commissions, public & private boards and committees. Study the system and its infrastructure. Find the city charter of your city or state and the rules that govern each of the institutions.
- How are these offices funded and by whom?
- Who are the top administrators?
- Who are the committee chairs?
- What is the sphere of influence of each of the institutions?

The Municipal Organization Chart for Baltimore City is an example of the hierarchy of a local political system.

Municipal Organization Chart for Baltimore City

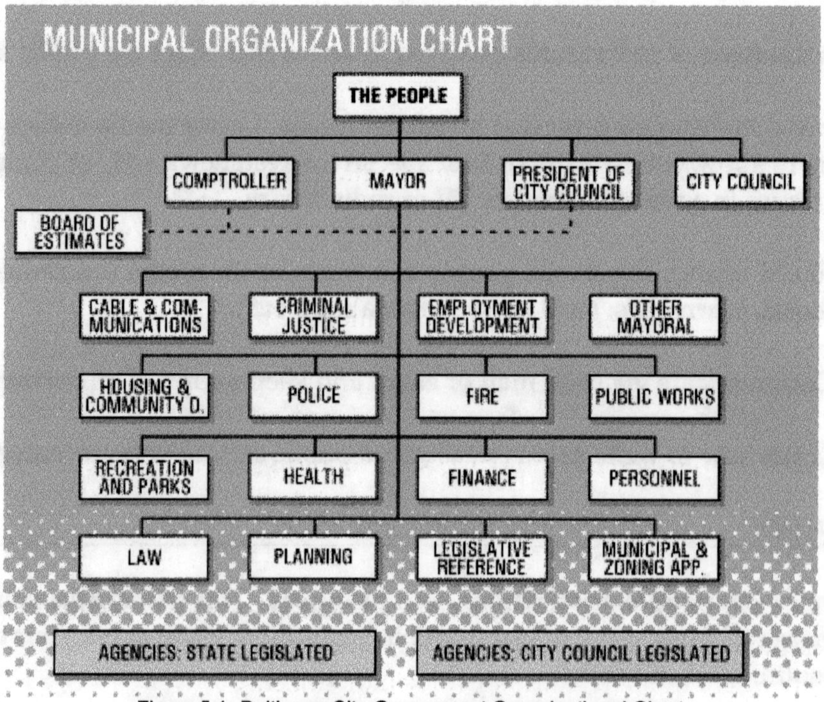

Figure 5.1: Baltimore City Government Organizational Chart

☞ **Resources**

A resource is a source of supply, support, or aid, especially one that can be readily drawn upon when needed. This includes land, labor, money, and other less tangible resources. Find out the following:

- What projects receive public funding?
  Are they social service projects, construction companies, consultants, educational support, consulting services and/or community programs?

- Who provides the support for these institutions and projects?

STEP 3: INVOLVEMENT

Getting involved is easier than you think. Attending meetings of these institutions is the first and easiest step. Most meetings are open to the general public. You can find out meetings dates, times, and locations from the office or institution. You may be interested in attending meetings of the city council, school board, county commissioners and other public meetings.

- Find out what is permissible at the meeting before you attend. (i.e. can you ask questions, record the meeting, etc.)

- Takes notes and pay attention to detail

Join community and political organizations, serve on boards and committees, or run for office in your local district or student government. It is not important that you have a position in the organization. A better tactic is to influence those with seats on the board to vote your way on the issues.

STEP 4: SYSTEMIC ISSUES & POLITICAL SOLUTIONS

A systemic issue is an issue that directly or indirectly is impacted by public policy, leaders and/or resources. However, political solutions should focus on policy, law, and actual facts, not emotion or opinion.

Example of Political Solution Strategy

In Baltimore, Maryland, the historic Memorial Stadium that was once home to the Baltimore Orioles and the Baltimore Colts, was scheduled for demolition to make way for a new facility.

The Opposition - the Maryland Historical Society and other concerned citizens did not want the building destroyed. The stadium was seen as a local landmark and a part of Baltimore history.

The Proponents - felt that the community would benefit from city development. The site would be developed by the nonprofit Govans Ecumenical Development Corporation for redevelopment into a housing complex for senior citizens.

The Answer - The Maryland Stadium Authority (MSA) - Now, if the MSA is owned by the people and they have a board who governs it, then what does that suggest? What is the political solution to the future problems? Is it holding a campaign in protest of destroying the landmark?

The Solution - After numerous protests by the Maryland Historical Society the state was forced to come up with a compromise. The Maryland Stadium Authority ratified an agreement on June 28, 2001, under which the lettered facade of Memorial Stadium would be kept intact as city-owned property. The state's contract with Potts and Callahan to demolish the stadium was amended to add about $1 million to the original $2.5 million cost. The authority hired a consultant and contractor to give advice on how to stabilize and support the 10-foot-high wall. Under the agreement between the state and the city, the memorial wall will be maintained by the city after the site is turned over.

STEP 5: ORGANIZE A COALITION

It is important to organize a community-based coalition to address systemic issues and develop political solutions. A coalition, or group of concerned citizens, should consist of no more than 10 members, who all understand true political activism. Coalition members must be honest, committed, and patient and understand that politics is a process.

Politics is not personal--there are no permanent allies and no permanent enemies. In order for the coalition to effectively address issues, it does not have to march or fight in the streets, but confront issues on the basis of information and the use of effective systemic and political strategies.

Organize political screening processes and candidates nights. This is when candidates come to a round table meeting organized by you to empress upon you what it is that they are going to do for the community. The goal is to build a relationship with these people and to find out what they are about and willing to support. With a network like the one mentioned above, you could nearly control the flow of policy in your local community and abroad. All of these strategies have been tried and proven, however, politics is an ever-evolving system, so be creative and bring new ideas to the process.

The government is an institution, and that institution is made up of boards, committees, commissions, and councils, which are made up of people. These institutions distribute resources and develop policies and laws--become a player in the game.

CHAPTER 6 REVIEW QUESTIONS

1) What is the first step to political activism? Why is this important?

_____

_____

_____

2) Why is it important for youth to get involved in politics?

_____

_____

_____

3) What are the three things you need to identify in step 2 of political activism?

•   _____

•   _____

•   _____

4) Name one way you can get involved in political activism.

_____

5) Political solutions should be based on _____,

_____, and _____   _____ ---

not emotion or opinion.

CHAPTER 6 ACTIVITIES

1. Register to vote
This is the easiest thing to do. Just register! Refer to page 101 for locations in your city where you can register to vote or register to vote online at: **http://www.rockthevote.org**

2. Investigate
Subscribe to a local newspaper and a national newsmagazine or newspaper.

National News
•   New York Times (http://www.nytimes.com)
•   Washington Post (http://www.washingtonpost.com)
•   Wall Street Journal

National & International News
  - Final Call Newspaper and Website (http://www.finalcall.com)
  - US News & World Report

3. Identify

Go online and do a search for "YourCity Government." Most states have websites with a ".gov" suffix. For example, Baltimore City's website is **http://www.ci.baltimore.md.us/government/**. Find the section that gives the municipal departments of your city. Take note of who controls what in your locale. Pick one office and identify the names and affiliations of all members. Some common departments or offices you may find are:

• Mayor's Office	• Finance Department
• Comptroller's Office	• Planning Department
• City Council	• Law Department
• Office of Employment	• Recreation & Parks
• Fire & Police Departments	• Public Works
• Health Department	• Housing

4. Involvement

Go to the next meeting of your local city council and answer the following questions.

a) Who facilitated the meeting? How was the meeting conducted?

_____

_____

_____

b) What issues were discussed at the meeting?

_____

_____

_____

c) Did any of these issues directly or indirectly effect you, your family, your church or school? How?

_____

_____

_____

5. Get involved with your local youth council

Contact your mayor's office and ask them if they have a city youth council. Find out when their meetings are held and how you can get involved. If they don't have one, ask what municipal department or office is addressing youth issues in your city.

CHAPTER 6 PROJECTS

1. Run for office in your Student Government or University Senate or volunteer for a friend's campaign. – OR – Volunteer for a local city council, congress, or mayoral campaign.

a) How difficult was it to gain interest for your campaign?

_____

_____

_____

b) Did you or your candidate win? What did you learn from this experience?

_____

_____

_____

2. **Coordinate a voter registration drive at your school.**
Contact your local election board to obtain voter registration applications and cards. Most offices will require representatives from your organization to attend a short training session before conducting the voter registration drive.

a) Was your campaign successful? Why or why not?

_____

_____

_____

b) How many people did you register to vote? _____

c) What activities, if any, were planned as a result of the registration drive?

_____

_____

_____

3. **Personal Leadership Plan: Part V -** Use what you learned about goal setting to form a plan for your political development.

Personal Leadership Plan: Part V

Political Development Goal(s): _____

_____

_____

_____

What has stopped me from accomplishing this goal?

_____

_____

Objectives - *What do I have to do in order to meet my overall goal?*

• _____

• _____

Action Items - *What steps will I take to fulfill my short-term goals?*

• _____

• _____

• _____

Outcomes - *What happened as a result of your action plan?*

• _____

• _____

Evaluation - *Did I meet my goal? How can I improve my approach in the future?*

_____

_____

SUGGESTED READING FOR CHAPTER 6

1. Torchlight for America by Minister Louis Farrakhan

2. Behold a Pale Horse by William Cooper

3. Teen Power Politics: Make Yourself Heard by Sara Jane Boyers

4. Black Power: The Politics of Liberation by Kwame Ture (Stokely Carmichael)

5. From Plan to Planet: The Need for Afrikan Minds and Institutions by Haki R. Madhubuti

CHAPTER 7:
TECHNOLOGICAL
DEVELOPMENT

TOPICS IN TECHNOLOGICAL DEVELOPMENT

- Why Technology is Important
- Technology in Business & Education
- Identifying Technology
- Access to technology

CHAPTER 7: TECHNOLOGICAL DEVELOPMENT

TOPICS IN TECHNOLOGICAL DEVELOPMENT
- Why Technology is Important
- Technology in Business & Education
- Identifying Technology
- Access to technology

 ## Key Terms for Technological Development

1. **COMPUTER** an electronic device designed to accept data, perform mathematical and logical operations at high speed, and display the results

2. **DATABASE** a comprehensive collection of related data organized for convenient access, generally in a computer.

3. **EMAIL (ELECTRONIC MAIL)** messages from one individual to another sent via telecommunications links between computers or terminals

4. **HTML (HYPERTEXT MARKUP LANGUAGE)** a set of standards used to tag the elements of a hypertext document, the standard for the World Wide Web.

5. **HTTP (HYPERTEXT TRASNFER PROTOCOL)** a protocol for transferring hypertext documents, the standard protocol for the World Wide Web

6. **HYPERTEXT** a method of storing data through a computer program that allows a user to create and link fields of information and retrieve data

7. **INTERNET** a large computer network linking smaller computer networks worldwide

8. **MEDIA** 1. an agency by which something is accomplished, conveyed, or transferred 2. a means of mass communication, such as newspapers, magazines, radio, or television.

9. **SEARCH ENGINE** a website that reports information available on the Internet.

10. **SPREADSHEET** software with a visual display of a worksheet *(used for financial plans, budgets, etc.)*

11. **TECHNOLOGY** the practical application of science to commerce (business)

12. **URL (UNIFORM RESOURCE LOCATOR)** the protocol for addresses on the Internet.

13. **WEBPAGE** a single, usually hypertext document on the World Wide Web that can incorporate text, graphics, sound, etc.

14. **WEB SITE** a connected group of pages on the World Wide Web regarded as a single entity, usually maintained by one entity and devoted to one single topic

15. **WORD PROCESSING** writing, editing, and production of documents, as letters, reports, and books, through the use of a computer program

16. **WWW (WORLD WIDE WEB)** a system of extensively inter-linked hypertext documents: a branch of the Internet

---

WHY TECHNOLOGY IS IMPORTANT

There is technology everywhere. Your calculator, fire alarm, microwave, and telephone are all examples of technological advancements. Technology is all around us, and is a part of our ever-evolving world. There are some misconceptions about technology that you, your family, or friends may have that can hinder you from advancing in this area.

COMMON MISCONCEPTIONS

- **Technology is Very Hard**

    Some people think that technology is very difficult. The fact is technology is common sense. Most people that know how to use computers and even do some of the more difficult programming will tell you that they learned from experience. Don't be intimidated by the computer or any other form of technology. The only way you can learn is to actually sit down and experiment.

- **I Don't Need Computers**

    As technology advances more rapidly each day, using computers is crucial to your success. You will find that most jobs require computer skills, from working in a warehouse to entry-level customer service positions. If you cannot use a computer, you are behind. If you do not feel comfortable using a computer you should make it a priority to deal with that issue. Take a class in keyboarding or using some common computer applications to get acquainted with the computer.

- **Technology is for "Techies" Only**

    The myth of the "computer nerd" is of the past. Nowadays, everyone uses computers. While everyone has different degrees of expertise and varying needs for the use of computers, using technology is not isolated to a group of elite individuals. In fact, most manufacturers work hard to make programs easy-to-use for the everyday person.

THE DIGITAL DIVIDE

The Digital Divide is a dynamic that is taking place in many countries around the world. The data shows that large gaps remain for Blacks and Hispanics when measured against the national average Internet penetration rate (Blacks 23.5% penetration rate, Hispanics 23.6%, compared to 41.5% nationally). The discrepancy of Internet and computer usage between minority communities and the mainstream population is alarming, but it is a problem that can be solved. Accessing resources for technological development and knowing what to do with those resources are the most important issues facing our communities. The only way to really learn about technology is through hands-on experience. For this reason, this chapter only seeks to provide you with awareness of the issues in technological development and provide you with access to those resources that will aid you in your development. As we emerge as leaders in our communities, we will be expected to have a healthy knowledge of technology. If we do not, we will surely be left behind.

Copyright © 2001 New Light Leadership Coalition, Inc.   *All Rights Reserved*

TECHNOLOGY IN BUSINESS & EDUCATION

The most common uses of technology are in business and education. Schools and businesses use technology and computers to help them function. No matter what profession you choose, you will be expected to have some level of computer knowledge. Most jobs require you to use a computer on a daily basis, especially entry-level positions. Most computers come with a basic software package that will include the following types of programs:

WORD PROCESSORS

Word processors are used for writing, editing, and production of documents, such as letters, reports, and books through the use of a computer program. This software replaced older machines such as typewriters and word processors. Businesses use word processors for letters, memos, reports, and other documents. Most students have used word processing software to compose homework assignments, reports, and essays. *Examples: Microsoft Word, WordPerfect, Claris Works*

SPREADSHEETS

A spreadsheet is a type of software that offers the user a visual display of a simulated worksheet. A spreadsheet is most commonly used for financial plans, budgets, charts, and tables. Spreadsheets have the capability to calculate numeric and statistical information by using formulas. *Examples: Excel, Microsoft Works*

DATABASES

A database is a comprehensive collection of related data organized for convenient access, generally in a computer. Databases are used to organize a large amount of information and have the ability to separate all of that information into reports. A report calls specific data requested by the user without having to view all of the data in the file. *Examples: Microsoft Access, Lotus Notes*

PRESENTATIONS

In the business world, speeches and presentations are commonplace. Delivering an effective speech can be more dynamic using presentation software. This is basically software that allows you to take important concepts, charts, and figures from a longer report or document and put them in a large format that can be displayed on the screen. Much like a slideshow, a presentation projects images so a small or large group can view your important points. *Examples: PowerPoint*

INTERNET BROWSERS

The Internet is used for many things such as chatting, email, and sharing information. Internet browsers allow you to view the websites displayed on the World Wide Web. Up-to-date information is at your fingertips making the Internet one of the easiest research tools to use. You must evaluate your sources to make sure they are credible. **Search engines** sometimes have bad outdated or can direct you to personal homepages. If a university, company, or other established source is not the host of the website, it may not be credible information. People post personal opinions online that may not be good for research. Be cautious of sites with very long **URLs** and too many advertisements. *Examples: Internet Explorer, Netscape*

ACCESS TO TECHNOLOGY

Even if you do not own a computer, there are many ways to access technology. Listed below are a few places you may want to go to learn about technology.

SCHOOLS

Some high schools have computer labs that you can use during your lunch hour and after school. Do not be afraid to take advantage of that resource and take some time to gain experience with the computer. Virtually all colleges and universities have computer labs that are accessible during the day and some that are open after hours. You may also want to look in the course catalog for an introductory computer course if you are not comfortable with using the computer.

LIBRARIES

Contact your local library to find out what types of technology they offer for research. Some libraries are equipped with computers that access the Internet, research databases, and word processing applications. Look in the phone book or online to get more information about computer classes offered by your local library and dates and times computers are available for use by the general public.

COMMUNITY CENTERS

Your local YMCA or recreation center may also provide access to computers and computer courses. Consult your phone book or the Internet to locate community organizations that have technology initiatives.

Copyright © 2001 New Light Leadership Coalition, Inc. *All Rights Reserved* Page 136

CHAPTER 7 REVIEW QUESTIONS

1. What are some common misconceptions about technology?

_____

_____

_____

2. What is the digital divide?

_____

_____

_____

3. Name two places you can go to gain access to technology if you do not own your own computer.

_____   _____

4. Which application would you use for the following projects:
    1 – Word processor 2 – Database 3 – Spreadsheet 4 – Presentation

    a) Term paper   1   2   3   4

    b) Budget   1   2   3   4

    c) Meeting Agenda   1   2   3   4

    d) Presentation for your boss   1   2   3   4

    e) Extensive data about the members of your organization   1   2   3   4

5. What is a good sign that an Internet source is not credible?

_____

_____

_____

Copyright © 2001 New Light Leadership Coalition, Inc.   *All Rights Reserved*

CHAPTER 7 ACTIVITIES

1. Sign up for a computer class at your local library or college. You can sign up for any class you would like to. If you do not know how to type, you should try to take a keyboarding class first before taking any other computer classes.

a) What computer class did you take?

_____

b) Did you find the class challenging or easy?

_____

_____

_____

c) Was the class helpful? Why or why not?

_____

_____

_____

_____

CHAPTER 7 PROJECTS

1. 💻 *WWW Activity:* Create your own website. You may want to use a free service that makes it easy for you to build your own personal website. Examples of free webhosting services are www.angelfire.com and www.tripod.com. These services usually take you step-by-step through the process of building a website and simplify it for everyday users. Follow the instructions on either of these sites, or do a search online for "free webhosting services" and use one of them to make your first website!

2. 💻 *WWW Activity:* Go to www.nsbe.org to get more information on issues that affect minorities in the technology field from the National Society of Black Engineers (NSBE).

3. **Personal Leadership Plan: Part VI -** Use what you learned about goal setting to form a plan for your technological development.

Personal Leadership Plan: Part VI

Technological Development Goal(s): _____

_____

What has stopped me from accomplishing this goal?

_____

Objectives - *What do I have to do in order to meet my overall goal?*

• _____

• _____

Action Items - *What steps will I take to fulfill my short-term goals?*

• _____

• _____

Outcomes - *What happened as a result of your action plan?*

• _____

• _____

Evaluation - *Did I meet my goal? How can I improve my approach in the future?*

_____

_____

SUGGESTED READING FOR CHAPTER 7

1. Microsoft® Office 2000 9 in 1 For Dummies® Desk Reference by Idg Publishing

2. Typing and Keyboarding for Everyone by Nathan Levine

3. Complete Guide to Multimedia; The Essential Explanation of the Latest Technology by DK Publishing

4. Sams Teach Yourself HTML and XHTML in 24 Hours by Dick Oliver, Charles Ashbacher

CHAPTER 8: ORGANIZATIONAL DEVELOPMENT

TOPICS IN ORGANIZATIONAL DEVELOPMENT

- Leadership Styles
- Essentials for Starting an Organization or Project
- Staying Motivated

CHAPTER 8: ORGANIZATIONAL DEVELOPMENT

Key Terms for Organizational Development

1. **AUTHORITY** power to influence or command thought, opinion, or behavior

2. **CHOICE** the act of choosing among alternatives; selection

3. **DECISION** 1. the act of reaching a conclusion 2. the passing of judgment on an issue under consideration

4. **INFLUENCE** the act or power of producing an effect without apparent exertion of force or direct exercise of command

5. **MISSION STATEMENT** a statement reflecting the organization's core values and reason(s) for existing. It should capture what you do, why you do it, how you do it, and for whom you do it. A mission statement broadly addresses the current and future purpose(s) of your organization

6. **MOTIVATION** the psychological feature that arouses one to action; the reason for the action

7. **OBJECTIVE** clear, measurable goal that can be achieved in a short period of time

8. **OUTCOMES** are the positive differences the program makes in the lives of people and communities.

9. **POWER** ability to do or act; capability of doing or accomplishing something

10. **TEAM** a number of persons associated in some joint action

---

Copyright © 2001 New Light Leadership Coalition, Inc.   *All Rights Reserved*   Page 143

LEADERSHIP STYLES

 In leading an organization or project, there are different styles of leadership that are appropriate at different times. A leadership style is simply the way you lead the group. Do you want to make sure everyone stays on task and closely watch over the group or take a more supportive role, not making any decisions without feedback from the members? Deciding on which style to use is essential to effective leadership.

THE DICTATOR

The first leadership style is the dictator. Sometimes called the authoritarian, the dictator style of leadership is directive. Dictators delegate responsibility, structure the activities and plans for the organization, and tries to motivate others. This style of leadership usually asks for little or no input.

THE DEMOCRAT

The democratic leader is a group facilitator. Asking questions and initiating discussion among members to reach a consensus is the role of the democrat. The democrat does not dictate, but encourages others to take responsibility.

THE NON-DIRECTIVE

The non-directive leader does not do much at all. They will never make a decision for the group and wait for others to make the decisions. The non-directive leader wants others to step up and take initiative, and shows signs of approval and support to group members.

You may be able to think of times when each style of leadership is appropriate. An effective leader realizes when to use each style of leadership according to the needs of the group.

Copyright © 2001 New Light Leadership Coalition, Inc.   *All Rights Reserved*   Page 144

ESSENTIALS FOR STARTING AN ORGANIZATION OR PROJECT

In order to spearhead any project or organization, there are some essential tools necessary to ensure success. Just as an individual needs purpose to live a meaningful life, an organization needs a purpose and structure to give it life. Deciding how your new organization will function is a process. A good idea usually stops at being just that unless it is developed. This section will give you some tools to aid in the development of your idea.

MISSION & VISION

Developing a Mission Statement

The most basic mission statement describes the overall purpose of the organization. You may have an idea of what the organization will do, but until you put it on paper it is not clear and concise. The mission statement tells the those outside your organization why you exist. The mission should answer the "who, what, where, when, and why" of your organization.

Brainstorming is a good technique to come up with a mission that describes your organization. The following are some questions you may consider when trying to come up with your mission statement.

♦ What is the problem or need your organization will address?
♦ What makes your organization unique?
♦ Who will benefit from your organization?

Developing a Vision Statement

The vision statement includes vivid description of the organization as it effectively carries out its operations. What is the ideal outcome of your organization's activities? What is your long-term goal?

When writing your vision, visualize what your organization will have accomplished at the end of five or ten years. What noticeable difference have you made in your community? What will be the change in the people you serve after your organization exists for some time? Your vision is an ideal end picture of the results of your work.

> ### STEPS TO STARTING AN ORGANIZATION OR PROJECT:
>
> 1. **Determine Need** - (Who will have a need for what provide with your idea? What is new and different about it? Why is it needed?)
> 2. **Seek Advice** - Talk to others to gain insight on the potential of your idea. Gain support of a core group of individuals to serve as advisors and partners
> 3. **Develop a Mission** - What is the purpose?
> 4. **Set Goals & Objectives** - How will you fulfill your mission?
> 5. **How Will it Run?** - Set a standard for how your organization or project will be governed
> 6. **Create Awareness** - Your organization is no good if no one knows about it. Marketing through radio, newspapers, flyers, and word of mouth is essential to your success.
> 7. **Stay Consistent** - Evaluate your effectiveness periodically and re-evaluate old goals. Make sure you stay consistent in whatever you do.

STRATEGIC PLANNING

The difference between where we are and where we want to be is what we do to get there. Where we want to go is defined in our goals. What we do to get there are our objectives and action plans. Strategic planning is the process of analyzing where you are as an organization and what steps you need to take to move forward.

Goals and objectives are used to formulate an action plan. Refer to the goal setting model in Chapter 2. Keep in mind that goals are small steps in fulfilling the overall mission of your organization or project. When writing a goal, make sure that the goal is attainable within a year or a short period of time. Also check to make sure it is directly related to your mission. An objective is a measurable outcome of your activities. When planning for an organization, make deadlines of when each goal will be reached and assign responsibility to a team or committee to complete each task.

STRATEGIC PLAN FRAMEWORK

Goal	Objective	Responsibility	Timeline
What are we trying to accomplish?	*What are the measurable outcomes of our goal?*	*Who is responsible for the completion of this objective?*	*When will the goal be reached?*

Figure 8.1: Strategic Plan Framework

An effective way of gaining insights on your assets and liabilities is to perform a S.W.O.T. analysis. This is a common approach in strategic planning. A SWOT analysis (Strengths, Weaknesses, Opportunities, and Threats) can assist you in identifying areas for development and can be the basis of your overall strategy for future advancement. After completing your SWOT analysis, ask yourself these questions:

☑ What do I need to do to overcome the identified weaknesses in order to take advantage of the opportunities?

☑ How will I minimize my weaknesses to overcome the identified threats?

☑ How can I use my strengths to enable me to take advantage of the opportunities I have identified?

☑ How can I use these strengths to overcome the threats identified?

Sample SWOT Analysis	
Strengths • Solid Membership • Successful fund-raising • Experienced and dedicated executive board	**Weaknesses** • Lack of priority on budget • Lack of financial planning • Not enough members to support expanding project goals.
Opportunities • Partnerships with other groups • Expansion of current programs	**Threats** • Unanticipated costs • Increasing project management needs

Figure 8.2: Sample SWOT Analysis

BYLAWS

Your bylaws, or constitution, explain how your organization functions. If you are starting an organization on campus, more than likely you will be required to submit a constitution to the Student Government Association for review. Without an accurate governing document, your organization will not function properly. It is important to consider your current capabilities and future goals when drafting your bylaws. Also keep in mind that bylaws are a guideline for how the organization runs and should not be just a document that collects dust and is never reference. Bylaws can be changed to adjust to developments within the organization and should always reflect how the organization is actually run. Review the sample bylaws on the following pages for a general idea of what your bylaws should include.

SAMPLE BYLAWS OF MY NEW ORGANIZATION, INC.

ARTICLE I - NAME
1. The name of the organization shall be [NAME].

ARTICLE II - PURPOSES
The following are the purposes for which this organization has been organized: [DESCRIBE]

ARTICLE III - MEMBERSHIP
Membership in this organization shall be open to all who [DESCRIBE].

ARTICLE IV - MEETINGS
This organization shall meet on the _____ day of each [MONTH] at [LOCATION]. The presence of not less than ____ (ex., 2/3) of the members shall constitute a quorum and shall be necessary to conduct the business of this organization.

ARTICLE V - VOTING
At all meetings, except for the election of officers and directors, all votes shall be by voice. For election of officers, ballots shall be provided and there shall not appear any place on such ballot that might tend to indicate the person who cast such ballot.

ARTICLE VI - BOARD OF DIRECTORS (EXECUTIVE BOARD)
The business of this organization shall be managed by a Board of Directors (Executive Board) consisting of [#] members. The directors to be elected on an annual basis. Vacancies in the Board of Directors shall be filled by a vote of the majority of the remaining members of the Board of Directors for the balance of the year.

ARTICLE VII - OFFICERS
The initial officers of the organization shall be as follows: President, Vice President, Secretary, and Treasurer.

The President shall preside at all membership meeting and act as Chairman of the Board of Directors (Executive Board).

The Vice President shall in assist the President in his or her duties and assume the role of President in his or her absence.

The Secretary shall keep the minutes and records of the organization.

The Treasurer shall handle all monies belonging to the organization and shall be solely responsible for such monies or securities of the organization.

Officers shall by virtue of their office be members of the Board of Directors.

SAMPLE BYLAWS OF MY NEW ORGANIZATION, INC. (CONTINUED)

ARTICLE VIII - STANDING COMMITTEES
The Board of Directors shall appoint all committees and their term of office shall be for a period of one year. Standing committees may be terminated by the action of the Board of Directors.

The standing committees shall be: [DESCRIBE]

ARTICLE IX - DUES
The dues of this organization shall be $ _____ per year and shall be payable on [DATE].

ARTICLE X - AMENDMENTS
These Bylaws may be altered, amended, repealed or added to by an affirmative vote of not less than _____ (ex. 2/3) of the members.

These Bylaws were approved by the Board of Directors of My New Organization, Inc. on June 22, 2002.

Figure 8.3: Sample Bylaws

COMMITTEES & MEETINGS

An organization should be comprised of committees with specific goals that relate to the mission or purpose of the organization. Each committee, or team, is comprised of members who are committed to the organization and have an understanding of why the organization exists and how it functions. Committee chairs should be carefully chosen. Oftentimes, the Board of Directors or Executive Board of the organization will chair certain committees.

Role of the Committee Chair
The Committee Chairman is the team leader of all committee work. The chair must be organized and know how to organize--both programs and people. He or she must know how to involve others and motivate them to do the work of the committee. Other responsibilities of the chair include: preparing and presenting committee reports to the organization, training a new committee chair when necessary, facilitating meetings, and soliciting input from all committee members.

Signs of a Good Committee
- Purpose of the committee is clear to all.
- An informal relaxed atmosphere.
- The chair and members are well informed and prepared.
- Interested and committed members.
- Meeting minutes are complete and accurate
- The work of the committee makes a valuable contribution to the organization.

Copyright © 2001 New Light Leadership Coalition, Inc.   *All Rights Reserved*

Committee Goals
Each committee is expected to fulfill a specific goal or objective during the course of a year. Below is a sample committee planning worksheet:

Committee Planning Worksheet

Committee Name_____

Goal 1: _____Deadline for Completion: _____

Goal 2: _____Deadline for Completion: _____

Goal 3: _____Deadline for Completion: _____

Committee Meetings *(When will your committee meet? Example: First Wednesday of Every Month)*

_____

Names of Committee Members:

_____   _____

_____   _____

_____   _____

Figure 8.4: Committee Planning Worksheet

Meetings
　　　　Meetings are the ongoing activities where members conduct the business of the organization. The Executive Board as well as each committee should conduct meetings on a regular basis. Meeting structure is important to running a smooth and productive meeting.

Parliamentary Law
Parliamentary law is a series of rules that were formulated to facilitate the transaction of business in meetings and are generally called the "Robert's Rules of Order." Parliamentary law is designed to help organizations conduct business in a timely and orderly fashion. The basics of parliamentary law involve equal rights of each member to discuss and debate issues, and the process of decision-making with majority vote decisions. A time limit is also prescribed to each segment of the meeting.

Qualities of an Effective Meeting
☑ Each individual's feelings and ideas are respected
☑ There is a feeling of collective responsibility
☑ Expectations are high
☑ Time is used efficiently
☑ Members exert a high level of effort
☑ Members feel that they can rely on one another

Sample Meeting Agenda

New Organization, Inc.
Executive Committee Meeting

Date: January 19, 2002   **Time:** 5:00pm - 6:00pm   **Place:** Conference Room

Ice Breaker – All new members and visitors introduce themselves.

I.   **Approve Meeting Minutes** – Meeting minutes from previous meeting are reviewed and approved.

II.   **Committee Reports** – Each committee chair and officer of the board reports to the general body.

III.   **Unfinished Business** – Progress reports from designations assigned at previous meeting.

IV.   **New Business** – Discussion of current projects and new ways to move forward on them. Also, new projects may be discussed during this time.

V.   **Announcements** – Members have the opportunity to discuss interesting news and upcoming events. The date and time for next meeting should also be announced.

VI.   **Adjourn** – Motion to adjourn meeting.

Figure 8.4: Sample Meeting Agenda

Tips for Ending a Meeting

☞ Ask each person for one thing that they learned during the meeting.

☞ Revisit action items and assignments and confirm due dates.

☞ Ask each person to share one action they will take in the next week as a result of the team session.

⚡ 10 Ways to Kill an Organization

1. Don't go to meetings.

2. If you do attend meetings, always arrive late.

3. Find fault with the work of the officers and members.

4. Never accept a position, as it is much easier to criticize than to do things.

5. Get upset if you are not appointed to a committee, but if you are, do not attend committee meetings.

6. If asked by a leader in the organization to give your opinion on some matter, tell them you have nothing to say.

7. After the meeting, tell everyone how things should have been done.

8. Do nothing more than what is absolutely necessary.

9. When other members use their ability to help matters along, say that a clique is running the organization.

10. Do not pay your dues

CREATING AWARENESS

So you started an organization, now what? What you want to do will be no good if no one knows about it. Get the word out about your new program to the community you plan to serve. There are many different ways to create awareness about your organization in the community.

Advertising: Utilize newspapers and radio stations to advertise your meetings and events. Do some research and find out what organizations are doing similar work and how they reach the public. If you are advertising on a small scale, such as in your school or neighborhood, flyers may be the best way to get the word out about your activities. If you have plans for growth, you should think about having a website. This automatically makes you global, because the Internet has no borders. No matter what way you advertise, remember you are putting out an image and message every time your name is out there. Be careful about how and where you advertise and make sure it is appropriate for the audience the advertisement is expected to reach. For example, you would not advertise a program for senior citizens in a college newspaper. Advertisements in some newspapers and in programs of local events are usually reasonably priced and are a good way to get the word out about what you are doing.

Mailing Lists: Build a mailing list, both snail mail and email, by collecting information from everyone that attends your meetings of functions. Make sure you have the consent of the individual or organization before placing their name on your mailing list. At every event and meeting you have, you should collect information from attendees. At the most basic, get a name, phone number, and email address.

Visibility: Partner with other organizations to sponsor events. This will get your name out and show that you support similar causes and organizations. Make sure you are visible at events that serve your constituents.

Press Release: Use a press release to get information out about your program or organization. You can send press releases to newspapers, magazines, TV stations, radio stations, and email lists. Your release should grab the reader's attention, which is more difficult than you think, considering the overload of information editors, reporters, and readers face on a daily basis. Make sure your topic has a "cat eats dog" appeal so it will not be immediately discarded. Press releases should provide the basics and give the reader a way to contact you. Be sure to include a your website address, if you have one, or somewhere else the reader can go for more information about your story.

Follow these guidelines when writing your press release:

- Ask yourself, "Is this story interesting enough for the news and who would be interested in it?"

- Tell the audience why the information is for them and give them a reason to continue reading

- Give the information first and then clarify the source, not vice versa

- The first line of your press release should be attention-grabbing

- Press releases should not be verbose--stay away from using too many adjectives and descriptive language

- Cover who, what, where, when, why, and how of your story

- Include all contact information (phone numbers, email, website, fax, etc.)

Sample Press Release

FOR IMMEDIATE RELEASE
June 1, 1995
CONTACTS:
Jane Smith, Student - (510) 268-1100
Tamara Schwarz, The Center for Commercial-Free Public Education
(510) 268-1100

STUDENTS AT DERRY MIDDLE SCHOOL CALL ON SCHOOL BOARD TO UNPLUG CHANNEL ONE

On Monday, June 5th, a group of 10 students from Derry Middle School will testify at the local School Board meeting against Channel One, a 12-minute news program with advertisements which is broadcast daily in every Derry Middle School classroom.

"We don't believe in the commercialization of our education. The contract with Channel One is like selling the kids to corporations," explained Jane Smith, a Derry Middle School student. "We're asking the School Board to cancel its contract with Channel One and find a non-commercial alternative."

Smith and a group of Derry Middle School students have been advocating all year for an end to Channel One. They have conducted a survey of the entire student body, finding that 60% of the students want an alternative. They have also published an alternative newspaper to educate the other students.

* * *

WHAT: Students from Derry area Middle School testify at the School Board meeting, calling for an end to Channel One in their classrooms.
WHERE: Derry School District Administrative Building, Derry PA
WHEN: 7:00 PM June 5, 1995

Figure 8.5: Sample Press Release

STAYING MOTIVATED

With all of the things learned in this workbook, it is important to stay focused and motivated to achieve your goals. This is probably one of the most crucial parts of any plan--the follow-through. Sticking to what you set out to do is a fulfilling process that will make you feel successful at something. Think about it this way: If you cannot keep a promise to yourself, can you keep a promise to someone else? You are your first priority and you should make a commitment to self first. When you complete your goals, you will be able to look back with a since of accomplishment. Here are some reminders to help you stay motivated.

⇨   Visualization

   Keep the end result in mind. That is the most important part of staying motivated. Why are you doing what you are doing? Why is it important to you? Visualize yourself having completed your goal. With the outcome in mind, you will be inspired to continue to work on your efforts.

⇨   Chart Your Progress

   Small victories are steps on the way to accomplishing a bigger goal. Every time you meet one of your goals, chart your progress. Keep track of what you have done and stay determined to do what you have failed to do. Develop a journal of all of the great things you have done and look back on it in times of struggle. When you realize what you have completed, you will see how great you are and realize that you can do it all over again.

⇨   Treat Yourself

   When you meet those small goals, take the time to congratulate yourself. Treat yourself to something new you have wanted for a while. After all, you are worth it. Remember to enjoy and celebrate your accomplishments. If you do not, your path to success will seem like a hard journey that is not worth the trouble. Make your development process fun by rewarding yourself for meeting your goals.

⇨   Form a Support System

   No man or woman is an island. If we could all do everything all by ourselves, then communication would be unnecessary. Have your friends and family members be active participants in your goal setting process. If you begin to slip, you will have someone to fall back on. People form support groups all the time to deal with difficult situations. Instead of coming together in crisis, encourage your friends to help you do something positive with your life. Forming a support system may inspire those who are helping you to set their own goals and you can begin to help each other.

CHAPATER 8 REVIEW QUESTIONS

1. Leadership Styles.
    In each of the following situations, check which leadership style is appropriate —
    dictator [D], democrat [DM], non-directive [ND].

    a. Regular committee meeting   _____

    b. First meeting of a new organization   _____

    c. Executive Board meeting   _____

    d. Post-activity evaluation meeting   _____

    e. Introducing a project   _____

2. Name three things you need when starting a new organization.

    ▪ _____

    ▪ _____

    ▪ _____

3. What are some of the duties of a committee chair?

    _____

    _____

4. What are four of the ten ways to kill an organization?

    _____

    _____

5. How will you stay motivated to accomplish your goals?

    _____

    _____

    _____

CHAPTER 8 ACTIVITIES

1. Plan meeting agenda for the first Executive Board Meeting of a new organization.

Meeting Agenda

Organization Name: _____

Committee Name: _____ **Date:** _____

Time: _____   **Place:** _____

Agenda:

I.   _____

II.   _____

III.   _____

IV.   _____

V.   _____

VI.   _____

VII.   _____

---

2. You are starting a new community service organization with some of your friends at your school. A local elementary school needs tutors to help their students in different subject areas and you want to be able to help them through your new group. Write a mission statement for your organization that clearly explains the purpose of your new organization.

    Organization Name: _____

    Mission Statement: _____

    _____

3. On a separate sheet of paper or using your computer, write a press release about your new program from Activity 2. Make sure you cover who, where, what, when, why, and how and that your program is newsworthy. Identify 3 places where you will send your press release (i.e. TV Stations, Radio Stations, Newspapers, etc.).

Copyright © 2001 New Light Leadership Coalition, Inc.   *All Rights Reserved*

CHAPTER 8 PROJECTS

1. 🖥 *WWW Activity:* Go to **http://www.innonet.org.** Sign up for their free project development service and use it to plan your next activity.

    a) Was this website helpful in planning your project? Why or why not?

    _____

    _____

    _____

    b) Did you find it difficult to clearly define your project goals and objectives?

    _____

    _____

    _____

    c) Will you use this tool in the future? Why or why not?

    _____

    _____

    _____

2. 🖥 *WWW Activity:* Add your organization to NLLC's Youth Empowerment Directory by going to **http://www.nllc.org**. Scroll down to the bottom and click on the 'Add your organization' link.

3. **Start an NLLC-Affiliated Leadership Council on Your Campus!**
   Are you a young leader that wants to become involved with NLLC? Take the initiative of leadership and start an NLLC-Affiliate Leadership Council at your school!

   Who is Eligible to Start a NLLC Leadership Council?
   Motivated and energetic NLLC members and organizational affiliates with an active representative.

   How do I Start a Council?
   1) Read over the Leadership Council Affiliation Packet. Affiliation Packets can be requested from NLLC by emailing info@nllc.org or calling 1.866.NLLC.INC. You can also go online to http://www.nllc.org/members to download the affiliation

packet. Please note you must fill out the online membership application before accessing the members' only website.

2) Find at least 2 other committed students on your campus to assist with founding the council

3) Gain the support of a faculty advisor

4) Contact NLLC headquarters with any questions

5) Submit the following for approval:

- NLLC Leadership Council Affiliate Application Form
- Membership Applications for founding members
- Constitution

Benefits of Starting a Leadership Council
- Local affiliates benefit from NLLC's national level networking and resources.
- Members receive discounts on NLLC publications and conferences.
- Belonging to a national organization provides a structure of continuity and prestige beneficial to a local affiliate.
- NLLC helps local affiliates get started serves as advisors for local affiliates.
- The NLLC Speaker's Bureau is available to local affiliates for help with program planning.

SUGGESTED READING FOR CHAPTER 8

1. Great Quotes from Great Leaders Career Press, Inc.

2. The Art of War by Sun Tzu

3. Robert's Rules of Order: *The Classic Manual of Parliamentary Procedure* by Henry Martyn Robert, Judith A. Roberts

4. Youth Leaders Roundtable Agenda Published by New Light Leadership Coalition, Inc.

5. Youth Leaders Inspirational Quote Book: *What is Leadership to You?* Published by New Light Leadership Coalition, Inc.

LEADERSHIP ESSAY

Write a short essay on what leadership means to you.

_____

_____

_____

_____

_____

_____

_____

_____

_____

_____

_____

_____

_____

_____

_____

_____

_____

_____

_____

_____

_____

_____

_____

_____

_____

_____

_____

_____

YOUTH LEADERSHIP POST-TEST

Re-take the Leadership Test now that you have completed the Youth Leadership Development Workbook. Circle the number that corresponds with each statement. Be honest!

	Strongly Disagree	Disagree Somewhat	Agree Somewhat	Strongly Agree
I am comfortable with myself	0	1	2	3
I am a good listener	0	1	2	3
I am a confident person	0	1	2	3
I am self-motivated	0	1	2	3
I am organized	0	1	2	3
I am good at getting my point across	0	1	2	3
I am willing to take on new challenges	0	1	2	3
I am responsible	0	1	2	3
I am not afraid of change	0	1	2	3
People look to me for guidance	0	1	2	3
I can motivate others	0	1	2	3
I think positively	0	1	2	3
I have control of my life	0	1	2	3
I work well with others	0	1	2	3
I am an honest person	0	1	2	3
I have a sincere desire to help others	0	1	2	3
I am good at solving problems	0	1	2	3
I am a risk-taker	0	1	2	3
I follow through with my goals	0	1	2	3
I know my purpose in life	0	1	2	3
Now add up the numbers in each column to get your total score:	0	_____	_____	_____
Add the numbers to get your total score:	My Total Score_____			

Meaning of Score:

46 – 60 * You are a well-rounded individual well on your way to becoming a leader!

32 – 45 * You have the potential to become a great leader. There are some qualities you want to develop before you are ready to take on leadership roles.

0 – 31 * You may not think you are a leader now, but keep trying to develop your leadership skills. Continue to review the Youth Leadership Development Workbook to improve your leadership skills.

Copyright © 2001 New Light Leadership Coalition, Inc. All Rights Reserved

JOIN NLLC!

Join a network of young people dedicated to leadership development and making a change in the community!

New Light Leadership Coalition came into existence in August of 1998 through the minds of two young people who felt a need to manifest the leadership potential in youth. This organization is operated for youth, by youth, with guidance from our elders.

MISSION

The mission of **New Light Leadership Coalition, Inc.** is to empower minority youth to develop their leadership potential by focusing on the personal, educational, economic, social, political, and technological aspects of life. NLLC is a youth-governed organization that will become the vanguard in a new era of leadership by *teaching*, *training*, and *uniting* young leaders.

NLLC MEMBERSHIP & AFFILIATE BENEFITS:

Networking Opportunities with Youth & Community Leaders * Meet other youth and community leaders at our events, workshops, and through our email group.

Leadership Training Programs * Develop your leadership potential by attending year-round training programs on leadership development.

Access to Members Only Website * Keep in touch with other members through our members only website. This site features chat, interactive forums, resourceful links, & more.

Scholarship & Internship Opportunities * Visit our members only website to receive monthly updates on scholarship and internship offers around the country.

New Members Orientation Packet * Learn about our organization and the opportunities for committee membership and how to start a Leadership Council at your high school, college or university.

Subscription to HORIZON Newsletter * Stay updated on Coalition activities and read insightful articles about leadership. You can also submit your own stories, inspirational poems, and articles to the newsletter.

Volunteer Opportunities * Earn community service hours by volunteering at our conferences and training programs.

Opportunity to Submit YOUR Ideas & Proposals * Have a great idea? Let us know about it! We will accept and consider all ideas for activities and projects.

Listing in the NLLC Youth Empowerment Directory (Organizations Only) * Get the word out about your organization through our Youth Empowerment Directory. Use this guide to find out about organizations in your area that support youth development initiatives.

Free Email * (*your_name@nllc.zzn.com*)

Membership Card * Good for discounts on NLLC products & events

OFFICERS USE ONLY | Submitted to _____ ☐Approved ☐Rejected

New Light Leadership Coalition, Inc.
"Empowering Youth through Leadership Development"
PO Box 66305 - Baltimore, Maryland 21239-6305 - http://www.nllc.org

MEMBERSHIP APPLICATION

PERSONAL INFORMATION (COLLEGE STUDENTS ENTER PERMANENT ADDRESS)

YOUR NAME		SEX M F	DATE OF BIRTH / /19
STREET ADDRESS			APT./BOX#
CITY	STATE ZIP	HOME PHONE	

ORGANIZATION/CAMPUS INFORMATION

SCHOOL NAME	CLASSIFICATION (CIRCLE ONE) Fresh. Soph. Jun. Sen. Grad. N/A
ORGANIZATION NAME	MAJOR/DEGREE (ex. B.S. Political Science)
STREET ADDRESS	SUITE/BOX#
CITY	STATE ZIP
CAMPUS/OFFICE PHONE	FAX

MEMBERS' ONLY WEBSITE ACCESS (CHOOSE A PASSWORD)

EMAIL ADDRESS	PASSWORD

What are your skills & talents? _____

_____

_____

Why do you want to join NLLC? _____

_____

_____

Membership Options
Select one:
☐**Youth (16 to 25)** [$15 Annual Dues]
☐**Youth Group** [$50 Annual Dues]
☐**Community Organization** [$100 Dues]

Affiliations
☐**Friend** [$25 Donation]
☐**Sponsor** [$100 Donation]
☐**Benefactor** [$500 Donation]

Payment Options (Select one)
☐Check   ☐Money Order

Amount Enclosed: $_____

Please sign me up for the following committee(s):
Note: You must join at least one committee
☐Conference Committee
☐Communications Committee
☐Fundraising Committee
☐Programming Committee

Please send me more information on:
☐Volunteer Opportunities
☐Executive Board Membership
☐Leadership Training Programs
☐Speakers' Bureau
☐Annual Youth & College Leadership Summit

Organizations & Youth Groups Only
☐Please list our organization in the NLLC Youth Empowerment Directory

Return this form with membership dues for the year to: NLLC, ATTN.: New Membership, PO Box 66305, Baltimore, MD 21239-6305. Make checks and money orders payable to *New Light Leadership Coalition*.

Excellence in Leadership Awards

Each year, New Light Leadership Coalition will recognize one young person and one youth group for excellence in leadership through the **Youth Leader of the Year** and **Youth Group of the Year** awards. These awards will honor youth for applying the principles of leadership in their own lives and organizations.

Winners will be honored at our Annual Youth & College Leadership Summit during the closing ceremony. They will receive an award, a two-year membership to New Light Leadership Coalition, and the opportunity to sit on our advisory council. **All finalists will be featured on our website**.

APPLICATION PROCEDURES:

Youth Leader of the Year Award
Submit a **one-page essay** on the following topic: *What is leadership to you and how have you applied the principles of leadership in your life?*

Youth Group of the Year Award
Please write to us to request an application or apply online at
http://www.nllc.org/awards

Who is Eligible?
YOUTH LEADER OF THE YEAR AWARD - Youth ages 16 to 25 are eligible for this award.
YOUTH GROUP OF THE YEAR AWARD - Community youth groups and high school & college student organizations are eligible.

Entries will be judged on clarity, quality, creativity, & uniqueness.

Please submit essays and applications with your name, school name, address, phone number, and email address to:

NLLC
Excellence in Leadership Awards
PO Box 66305
Baltimore, Maryland 21239-6305

All applications must be postmarked by September 30. Finalists will be notified by November 1.

Youth Leader of the Year Award Application

Fill out the following application to enter the YOUTH LEADER OF THE YEAR AWARD competition. Please *type* in the fields below or fill out the application neatly in ink. Mail completed applications along with your essay and any supporting documents to **NLLC Excellence in Leadership Awards, PO Box 66305, Baltimore, MD 21239-6305.**

1. Contact Information	
Full Name	
Ethnic Origin	☐African American ☐Hispanic ☐Native American ☐Asian American ☐Other
Age	
Gender	☐Male ☐Female
College/University	
Permanent Address	
City, State, Zip	
Home Phone	
Email	

2. School Information	
Campus Address	
Address 2	
City, State, Zip	
Campus Phone	

3. Academic & Extracurricular Background	
Graduation Date	
Major Area of Study	
Classification	☐Freshman ☐Junior ☐Out of School ☐Sophomore ☐Senior ☐Graduate
Extracurricular Activities & Leadership Positions	1) Organization: Dates of Participation: Positions Held: 2) Organization: Dates of Participation: Positions Held: 3) Organization: Dates of Participation: Positions Held:
Awards & Honors	

Copyright © 2001 New Light Leadership Coalition, Inc.   All Rights Reserved

Work & Volunteer Experience	1) Company: Dates: Job Title: 2) Company: Dates: Job Title: 3) Company: Dates: 4) Job Title
References	Reference 1 Name: Reference 1 Number: Reference 1 Email: Reference 2 Name: Reference 2 Number: Reference 2 Email:

4. Short Answers

a. How would you define leadership?

b. Are you a leader? Explain

Please mail your essay and application to NLLC Excellence in Leadership Awards, PO Box 66305, Baltimore, MD 21239-6305.